Stray Reflections
by Jawad S. Mian

2020

For you
For who you are
For where you are
For where you want to go
For who you want to be

*And you?
When will you
begin that long journey
into yourself?*

— Rumi

About the Author

Jawad Mian is the founder of Stray Reflections, a global macro research firm. He is devoted to the pursuit of truth—in life and in markets. As the great poet Allama Iqbal wrote in his private journal in 1910, "I wandered in pursuit of my own self; I was the traveler, and I am the destination."

In this book, Jawad digs deep down into his personal experiences and shares not just insights on many important themes in life, but excerpts from great literature and the eternal wisdom of the great poets, saints, and philosophers. The series of articles show what he was experiencing in his own relationship to life and work when he wrote them.

Jawad's writing is prized for its staunch independence, distinct poise, clarity of thought, and courage to push readers outside the manacles of conventional thinking. He lives in Dubai with his wife, Saniha, and daughters, Zaynab, Fatima, and Maryam.

Stray Reflections

Contents

2014
The Opening — 15
The Fall — 20
The Shrine — 24
The Gospel of Wealth — 27
Bani Adam — 32
Grattitude — 34
Old School Macro — 36
Zaynab — 42
Musicology — 45
The Elegant Universe — 48
The Reader — 52
The Return — 56

2015
Dreams Deferred — 59
The Forty Rules of Love — 63
The Bridge Builder — 65
The Fault in Our Stars — 67
Culture of Complaint — 70
Eyes Wide Shut — 72
The Sixth Sense — 76
The Holiday — 79
Saving the World — 81
I Am — 83
The Resistance — 87
Remembering Christmas — 90

2016

Blasphemy	93
Wisdom from Emerson	98
The Party	102
Bilaliwood	103
The Pilgrimage	106
The Greatest	109
Dope	113
What Babies Teach Us	116
Shibumi	119
The Seeker	122
The Big Short	126
The Present	130

2017

Great Expectations	133
The Art of Stillness	136
The Woods	139
Abundance	142
Wonder Woman	144
Wajd	151
The Conference of the Birds	153
The Impostor	156
Nature	159
When Breath Becomes Air	161
Live the Questions	167
The Divine Creation	170

2018

The Corporation	175
The Feast	181
DAMN	183
Evolve	186
The Writing Life	190
Deep Work	193
The Unknown	196
The Walk	200
The Concrete System	209
The Hikam	215
Entropy	217
The Edge	219

2019

Opus Dei	223
Xinyi	224
Letting Go	227
The Saint	230
The Great Commandment	233
The Tragedy of Speed	235
An Ode to Silence	238
The Apology	242
The Entanglement	245
The End of our Time	250
The Dip	252
Memento Mori	255

2014

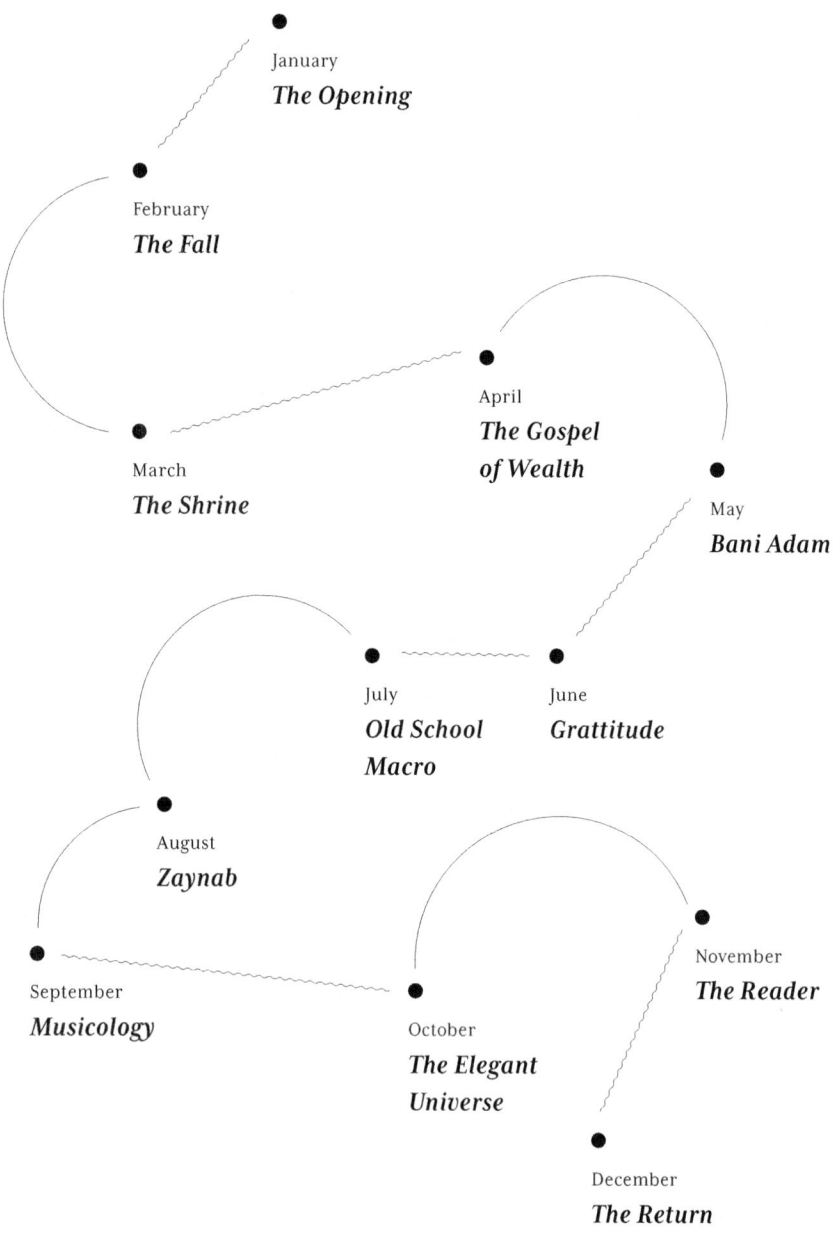

January
The Opening

February
The Fall

March
The Shrine

April
The Gospel of Wealth

May
Bani Adam

June
Grattitude

July
Old School Macro

August
Zaynab

September
Musicology

October
The Elegant Universe

November
The Reader

December
The Return

The Opening

I'd like to tell you a story.

By 2006, it had been four years since I had last visited Pakistan. I was twenty-two and change, and I had kept myself busy in Toronto with a work-and-study routine that had not allowed me to travel anywhere. But thankfully, my eldest brother was getting married there in August, and I was really looking forward to going back. I had particularly wanted to spend time with my grandparents because they were aging quickly and I felt that I had so much to talk about with them. I wanted to learn more about the history of our family and country, hear stories about their childhood, their work and married life, and just learn from their experiences.

I still remember the night of March 18. I was in Canada when I got a message from home that Dada Abu had passed away (urdu for my grandfather from my father's side). I immediately broke down. All of the sudden, I felt so far away from all that really mattered. The news shook me hard. I think somewhere deep inside, this had been a fear of mine. I knew that Dada Abu was getting weaker, but I did not like to imagine that his life could end. Though I had not spent much time with him, I felt very attached, and in an instant, I was filled with regret at not having gone back to Pakistan earlier and speaking with him the way I had wished. Now, it was too late.

A couple of months later, my Nana Abu (my grandfather from my mother's side) came to Canada for a visit and to live with his son for a little bit. I promised myself that I was going to make the most of this opportunity and spend as much time with him as possible. Nana

Abu was used to praying in the mosque five times a day, a routine which was not possible during his time in Canada. So I decided that I would pick up my uncle and Nana Abu very early in the morning, and we would then pray fajr together in the mosque, pick up some breakfast from Tim Hortons, and then go for a walk by the lake before making my way to work.

As we watched the sun rise, I would press my grandfather with questions about his past. It was on these lovely, long morning walks that Nana Abu opened up and first started sharing his stories. I was hooked. Almost every day, I would return from work in the evening and head over to my uncle's apartment to spend time with Nana Abu and hear more about his life. Little by little, it dawned on me that I didn't want to forget these amazing stories and perhaps others in the family may not have heard them before either. With that in mind, I began jotting down his thoughts and life experiences.

My grandfather had no clue what I was up to. Slowly, my notes took the shape of short stories, and then, I got the idea to turn them into a little book that I could distribute to my extended family. The whole process, from beginning to end, took a little over a month. The book was edited and printed just a few days before I was going to leave for Pakistan to attend my brother's wedding.

To this day, giving that book to Nana Abu has been one of the most rewarding experiences of my life. I still vividly recollect his reaction. He had the most incredible smile on his face—he was beaming!

He said to me, "On the Day of Judgment, angels will hand us a book with a full list of our deeds in this world. You have given me that book right here, in this life, in this world." He made me sit next to him while he read the entire book from cover to cover. He laughed out loud, corroborated the stories told, and spent the evening entranced and full of joy. From that day onwards, the book would always be by his side. He would take it with him everywhere, like a prized possession, and never fail to tell people about it. Without a doubt, it brought him a tremendous amount of happiness.

Almost five years later, on an April morning in 2011, my Nana Abu passed away back in Pakistan. My last meeting with him was less than two months prior in February when I was in Islamabad for a short visit.

One afternoon during that stay, he called me into the study room, where he was engaged in a discussion with a friend. As I walked into the room, he raised his hand toward me and asked the gentleman if he knew who I was. The visitor hesitated to answer, and then Nana Abu proceeded to say, "He is Nusrat's son; he is the one who wrote that book about me." I could sense that he was very proud.

The following morning I went over to Nana Abu's room to say goodbye. I had lunch plans elsewhere and was not going to return. As soon as I spoke of my departure, he was disturbed. He was not feeling his best, and he grabbed me by the arm. It was Friday, and he asked me to take him to Friday prayers, saying, "I will feel stronger with you next to me." I told him of my lunch plan and tried to excuse myself. I reassured him that my young cousin would take him to prayers, like he always did, and that he would be just fine and that there was nothing to worry about. He did not want to hear it, so he asked again. Once more, I tried to find a way out. But Nana Abu was adamant and insisted yet again.

And then, at that moment, suddenly, I was overcome with an incredible sense of guilt. I couldn't believe that I was being so selfish. Thinking about it now, I still can't believe it took three attempts of him asking me before I decided to finally change my mind. How ridiculous! So a few hours later, we went together for Friday prayers along with my cousin. Nana Abu held my hand as we walked. We prayed and returned home right after. He thanked me, and I felt extremely ashamed. I kissed him as he got into bed to rest. That was the last time I saw him.

Of course, I did not think that would be our last meeting. And now, I imagine not having this memory of him. I would never have forgiven myself. I almost feel that Nana Abu purposefully exonerated me from life-long guilt by insisting repeatedly that I accompany him to Friday prayers. There is something to be said about that. I should have been the one thanking him.

As I reflect on my relationship with Nana Abu, I have much to be thankful for. But for me, the one thing that stands out the most—in terms of his contribution to my life—was that he inspired me to start writing. I discovered a passion for something I never knew existed.

Nana Abu was also the first person to introduce me to Allama Iqbal, the cosmic poet and spiritual godfather of Pakistan. I remember him telling me that we must strive to be Iqbal's *Shaheen*, or Eagle—his avian symbol that carries a number of inspiring features: courage, independence, self-respect, self-control, lofty thinking, character and honor, spiritualism over materialism, constant struggle and endurance, perseverance, purity of the soul, and passion. I did not understand the full weight of what he meant at the time. I do now.

Iqbal preached that one should take an active attitude toward life and talked of man's high purpose in the world. He had a moral stake in the social and political life of the people around him, motivated by the love for the ideal of the moral and spiritual regeneration of mankind. In the attainment of this ideal, he sacrificed everything. Parsing through his brilliant words, one can't help but feel a strong sense that the variety and richness of his ideas and thought are all the more relevant today in our turbulent times.

Iqbal was a voice from the East that found a common denominator with the West. He sought to inspire people through his writings—whatever their tongue, whatever their creed—with an element of protest against existing conditions, becoming a trendsetter for the coming generation of thinkers. His lyrical style was simple, direct, and forceful; and his concepts had universal appeal. He defined concrete proposals for building the future world along new lines.

The title of this book is taken from the private journal of the same name kept by Allama Iqbal in 1910. The journal contained odd jottings based on the impressions of the books he was reading at the time, his thoughts and feelings about the environment in which he lived, as well as quick and sensitive responses to many of the ideas and forces that were affecting him. Like Iqbal, "I wandered in pursuit of my own self; I was the traveler, and I am the destination."

In deep humility, I pay respect to my grandparents who stirred me up inside and opened my heart to Iqbal. Without their guidance, I would be oblivious to man's true nature and the secrets of the self. Now, I find myself gradually traveling from chaos to the cosmos along the journey of life. It is the Truth that I am after, and what I want to make apparent to fellow wayfarers on the path.

Praise be to God, at the beginning and at the end.

The Fall

> *Every adversity, every failure, every heartbreak, carries with it the seed of an equal or greater benefit.*
> — Napoleon Hill

I come from a big family. My mother has eight siblings, and my father has ten. You can imagine how many uncles, aunts, and cousins I have. Yet there is not a single lawyer, doctor, or engineer in our whole family. Not many finished university, and no one pursued a professional degree. And so, it was my father's wish to have at least one doctor in the family. Because I was "smarter" than my elder two brothers, I was the one encouraged to enter the medical profession.

I was sure that my personal calling was to be a doctor, and that was exactly what I was going to be. My friends started calling me Dr. Jawad, and I started watching ER and Doogie Howser. I planned my life. I was going to go to Johns Hopkins, get a medical degree, specialize in some difficult-to-pronounce discipline that involved surgery, and be set for life. Based on my research, I would be making six figures in six years.

And then, in grade eleven, when I was sweet sixteen, I sat for my O Level examinations. My parents were traveling, my two elder brothers were already studying abroad, and my younger brother was my younger brother—who cares about them? The point is, I was home alone for the very first time in my life. I started skipping school and could not be bothered about preparing for the important examinations. I was too busy discovering life.

This was an epic disaster.

Here's the results: I got an A in French, a B in English, a C in Physics, a D in chemistry, an N in math (to this day I don't know what "N" stands for), and an E in biology. That's right, Dr. Jawad got an "E" in O Level biology. My promising medical career was over. That was one of my first encounters with the "F" word. I was a big failure!

My parents could not believe their eyes when they saw my alphabet-soup-inspired report card. I had let them down—big time! To this day, there's still not a doctor in the family. After a crisis meeting with my father and eldest brother, it was decided that I would become a lawyer now, "Barrister Jawad Mian." Naturally, I started watching Ally McBeal.

Because of my colorful O Level grades, I was not willing to repeat the experience with my A Level examinations. So England was off the list as a destination for further studies. I decided to go to Canada and study finance during the prelaw years. My first year at college was great socially but pretty poor academically. There's one particular experience that may explain the entire episode.

I had an exam in the morning for which I had not studied a word. I played cards all night with friends and chatted on MSN messenger. My older brother came online, and we chatted. He asked what I was up to, and I expressed great stress about the exam in the morning. I pretended to be working really hard. His next words to me have stayed with me ever since. He said, "May you get what you deserve."

I immediately uttered the other "F" word. Based on my study ethic, I had no doubt I would fail my morning exam. I was right. That was a turning point for me. I thought about my parents, I thought about my O Level grades, and I thought about my attitude toward life.

I pulled my act together and got pretty decent grades after that. The highest score that I achieved in my final year was a ninety-three on a politics class. I only boast of that grade to prove that I'm not really that stupid. I finished my four-year finance degree in three years (perhaps the first serious sign of overambition). Looking for a change of scenery, I applied to a school in England to study law and got in.

Now, I faced a dilemma. I wasn't sure if I wanted to be a lawyer anymore. After much deliberation, I decided to defer my law school acceptance for a year and look for a job in finance—just to try it out. I soon landed a position as a bank teller, and just like that, my personal calling changed yet again. From doctor to lawyer to... hedge fund manager? The personal legend continues.

Life is a journey, and we are all just travelers. It's okay to fall down or not know where you're going. Nature has marked out a path for each of us, and it won't let us stray too far from our course. There is no shame in falling, only in failing to rise and get back up on our feet. As Paulo Coelho said, the secret of life is to fall seven times and to get up eight times. Even success, it has been well said, is nothing more than moving from one failure to the next with undiminished enthusiasm.

Life is not without its challenges. The critical test of humanity is how we lead our life and how we endure the challenges and trials that are inflicted upon us. As the perceptive nineteenth-century author Hannah Whitall Smith, wrote:

> The mother eagle teaches her little ones to fly by making their nest so uncomfortable that they are forced to leave it, and commit themselves to the unknown world of air outside. And just so

does our God to us. He stirs up our comfortable nests, and pushes us over the edge of them, and we are forced to use our wings to save ourselves from fatal falling. Read your trials in this light, and see if you cannot begin to get a glimpse of their meaning. Your wings are being developed.

So what if you fall?

How else will you learn to fly?

Oh Eagle!
Don't get frightened of these
Furious, violent winds,
These blow only to
Make you fly higher.

— Allama Iqbal

The Shrine

As fragrance abides in the flower,
As reflection is within the mirror,
So does your Lord abide within you,
Why search for him without?
— Guru Nanak

There is an old Hindu legend that has been recounted in many books. I stumbled upon it in William Danforth's *I Dare You!*

> At one time all men on earth were gods, but men so sinned and abused the Divine that Brahma, the god of all gods, decided that the godhead should be taken away from man and hid some place where they would never again find it to abuse it.
>
> "We will bury it deep in the earth," said the other gods.
> "No," said Brahma, "because man will dig down in the earth and find it."
> "Then we will sink it in the deepest ocean," they said.
> "No," said Brahma, "because man will learn to dive and find it there, too."
> "We will hide it on the highest mountain," they said.
> "No," said Brahma, "because man will some day climb every mountain on the earth and again capture the godhead."
> "Then we do not know where to hide it where he cannot find it," said the lesser gods.
> "I will tell you," said Brahma, "hide it down in man himself. He will never think to look there."

And that is what they did. Hidden down in every man is some of the Divine. Ever since then he has gone over the earth digging, diving and climbing, looking for that godlike quality which all the time is hidden down within himself.

So how do we find the Indwelling One?

Most of the world religions and spiritual traditions will tell you that the Way is not to be found in the sky above; the Way is in the heart. As Rabbi Abraham Joshua Heschel, one of the leading Jewish theologians and philosophers of the twentieth century, said, faith is an endless pilgrimage of the heart.

As simple as it sounds, the inner journey is not without effort. Our heart is a vessel that contains a debris of old memories, our secrets, our feelings, our dreams. But we also store up hard little stones of self-concern, anger, hatred, arrogance, and greed. A vessel must first be emptied before it can be refilled, such that, as Charles Le Gai Eaton observed, only someone who has expelled this debris from the heart can hope that something of the Divine plenitude may flow into him. When the heart is polished, all the impurities vanish, and our own unblemished essence is illuminated. It is of this purity that the Prophet Jesus probably spoke of when he said, "Blessed are the pure in heart for they shall see God."

Mahmud Shabistari, the thirteenth-century Persian poet, beautifully conveys this path to self-realization in the following verse:

> Go sweep out the chamber of your heart,
> Make it ready to be the dwelling place of the Beloved,
> When you depart out, He will enter,
> In you, void of yourself, will He display His beauties.

The shrine of God is in the heart of man. And so, the principal moral of religion is to consider the heart of others, so that in the pleasure and displeasure of every person with whom we come in contact, we can see the pleasure and displeasure of God. To Bulleh Shah, the eighteenth-century Sufi, this mattered more than anything else:

> Tear down the mosque, tear down the temple,
> Break everything in sight,
> But do not break anyone's heart,
> For that is where God resides.

The biggest loss in life is to have a hardened heart. We have let our hearts rust through years of neglect. If we could just rise above the ordinary faults of human life and see the Divine in our fellowman, we would take more care to guard our own attitude, speech, and action to prevent any undesirable impression from occupying our heart. For the wise—the clear-hearted ones—overlook the weakness in others because they see this weakness reflected as their own.

The Gospel of Wealth

Andrew Carnegie was once the richest man in the world. Coming from a poor background, he loved making money, and he loved spending it. Yet he felt guilty sometimes about loving it so much. In December of 1868, at the age of thirty-three, Carnegie sat at his desk at the St. Nicholas Hotel in New York and wrote a memo to himself. He had a net worth of $400,000 and received an annual income in dividends of $50,000 from his holdings in sixteen companies. He wrote the following:

> Beyond this never earn. Make no effort to increase fortune but spend the surplus each year for benevolent purposes. Cast aside business forever except for others. Man must have an idol—the amassing of wealth is one of the worst species of idolatry—no idol more debasing than the worship of money. To continue much longer overwhelmed by business cares and with most of my thoughts wholly upon the way to make more money in the shortest time, must degrade me beyond hope of permanent recovery.

He vowed to retire in two years. But the lure of wealth proved to be too strong. By 1901, he was easily worth over $250 million.

His conscience never slept. In a famous article titled "The Gospel of Wealth," which was published in 1889, Carnegie expressed that the chief problem of the age was the proper administration of wealth "so that the ties of brotherhood may still bind together the rich and poor in a harmonious relationship." Here's an excerpt:

This, then, is held to be the duty of the man of wealth: To consider all surplus revenues which come to him simply as trust funds, which he is called upon to administer in the manner which, in his judgment, is best calculated to produce the most beneficial results for the community. The millionaire's wealth was not his to spend, but his to wisely give away. Rich men should be thankful for one inestimable boon. They have it in their power during their lives to busy themselves in organizing benefactions from which the masses of their fellows will derive lasting advantage, and thus dignify their own lives.

But how do you determine what's "surplus" in today's world?

As of last year, the Swiss bank UBS estimates there are 2,325 billionaires around the world who have a combined net worth of $7.3 trillion. The average person in this ultra-affluent tier is 63 years old and has liquid holdings of $600 million. There is a wealth "ceiling" of $10 billion, with 95% of the world's billionaires worth between $1 billion and $10 billion. Crossing the $10 billion threshold has been particularly rare.

Based purely on subjective reasoning, we can probably all come to an agreement that anything above $1 billion represents a fair surplus. With interest rates at 2%, this would provide an annual income of $20 million, enough to indulge in a conspicuous amount of consumption. The world would still have 2,325 billionaires and nearly $5 trillion swept aside to spend for "benevolent purposes." A mere 1% of that sum could fund the basic health and education needs of the world's poorest people.

The point I'm trying to make here is really simple: there is enough money in this world to solve all of our problems. It's just that the money doesn't flow to all the right places. There is no shortage of food either. No one should sleep hungry. Yet food just doesn't flow over to where it's needed the most. As Gandhi once said, the earth provides enough to satisfy every man's need but not every man's greed.

How do we unclog this world?

An Oxfam study found that—based on current trends—by next year, 1% of the world's population will own more wealth than the other 99%. According to the report, eighty people now own the same amount of wealth as more than 3.5 billion people, which is down from 388 in 2010. This has sparked a futile debate on the situation of increasing global inequality and on the ways to correct such imbalances. I, for one, don't believe in a government's interjection or redistributive taxation. The laws of distribution should be as free as the laws of accumulation. We just need to break down our ego-shell and awaken our conscience. What we need is less capitalism and more humanism.

Peter Buffett, Warren Buffett's son, penned an op-ed for the *New York Times* in June of 2013 titled "The Charitable-Industrial Complex." In it, he wrote:

> As more lives and communities are destroyed by the system that creates vast amounts of wealth for the few, the more heroic it sounds to "give back." It's what I would call "conscience laundering"— feeling better about accumulating more than any one person could possibly need to live on by sprinkling a little around as an act of charity.

> But this just keeps the existing structure of inequality in place. The rich sleep better at night, while others get just enough to keep the pot from boiling over. Nearly every time someone feels better by doing good, on the other side of the world (or street), someone else is further locked into a system that will not allow the true flourishing of his or her nature or the opportunity to live a joyful and fulfilled life.

Excluding future pledges, billionaires, on average, donate just over $100 million cumulatively over their lifetimes. This is equivalent to 3% of their net worth. Why can't we give as extravagantly as we spend? And why do we wait till the end of our lives? Goethe said well, "Nobody should be rich but those who understand it." We all need to reflect on what it means to succeed in life and make the world a better place.

And this brings to mind an apt Emerson quote for our troubled times: "A whole generation adopted false principles, and went to their graves in the belief they were enriching the country they were impoverishing." Emerson proposed following nature regarding what each individual should do:

> In the order of nature, the benefit we receive must be rendered again, line for line, deed for deed, cent for cent, to somebody. Beware of too much good staying in your hand. It will fast corrupt and worm worms. Pay it away quickly in some sort. He is great who confers the most benefits.

I have come to realize that my earnings are not just my own. Mixed in my purse is the right of many others who earn too little or nothing at all. We are all but trustees for the poor and dispossessed. This is the real test for mankind. The river of money should always flow, with no forcing, no holding back.

What's your surplus?

> *I don't think there is such a thing as an intelligent mega-rich person. For who with a fine mind can look out upon this world and hoard what can nourish a thousand souls.*
>
> — Kabir

Bani Adam

> *For good or evil, we are a single people:*
> *the more we become conscious of this, the*
> *less difficult and long will be humanity's*
> *progress toward justice and peace.*
> — Primo Levi

The world is getting increasingly uncomfortable with the proliferation of race and religious tensions, internal conflicts, and sporadic terror attacks. There are more people displaced today than at any time since World War II. Divisive politics are exacerbating these trends by preventing action on the one hand while fueling hate, bigotry, and intolerance on the other hand.

Now more than ever, we must come together as *Bani Adam*, the "Children of Adam"—an aphorism by thirteenth-century poet Sa'adi that calls for the breaking of barriers preventing the progress of humanity as one and as a whole. Underneath the superficial differences and distinctions that have long been used to divide us, we all have the same fundamental needs, after all, for connection, purpose, and to matter in this vast universe.

"For one human being to love another," wrote Rainer Rilke, "that is perhaps the most difficult of all our tasks, the ultimate, the last test and proof, the work for which all other work is but preparation." If humanity is our race, love should be our religion. And although I admit that it's easy to love a perfect God and far more difficult to love fellow human beings—insecure and imperfect as we are—we must realize that all human beings, without exception, have a unique place among God's creation. "I breathed into him of My Spirit," He says in the Qur'an.

If there is any moral principle that we must understand, it is that humanity is as one single body, and each faith, all races are the different organs. The well-being of each of those organs determines the happiness and well-being of the entire body. Ask yourself just how often you feel strain throughout your body when just one organ is in pain.

Faced with overwhelming violence and suffering, we need to rediscover our Oneness.

> *We may be Muslims, Jews, or Christians. But until our hearts become the mould for every heart, we will see only our differences.*
>
> — Rumi

Grattitude

Artists have no choice but to express their lives. Peter Tunney is one such man. His life story is as colorful as his highly acclaimed art.

Tunney nearly died in a car accident at the young age of thirteen before he sprang back to life. He turned into a professional magician after he got out of the hospital, and he barely got through high school. He would go to college, only to be thrown out, and began selling cars in a dealership. He was invited to work on Wall Street, which he did successfully for a number of years, before getting bored and deciding to spend time in Africa as a photo curator instead. After ten years in the savannah, he still felt unfulfilled and started making art as a form of nourishment.

Speaking of his journey in one of his interviews, Tunney said, "I went to a party when I was thirteen and I came home when I was forty-three. I was running, trying to get stuff, accomplish things. When I got sober, I gave up all that. I just let the whole world come to me. And once I surrendered and let go of everything, good stuff happened to me."

Tunney's artwork imitates life. It shows you that when one door closes, another will open. You just have to remain calm and persevere. His thought was to create a body of work that would mirror his own life's experiences. Tunney captures everything: heaps of trash, scraps from his travels, pages from magazines, newspapers, books he's read, gifts from nature, old photographs, and giant impressions in his mind. He combines them all with bold typography into a massive collage or a mural using his inimitable perspective.

What I love most about Tunney's work is that he stands outside the conventional boundaries of art and design. He won't conform. I respect that. He watches only the trend of his inner need, which is reflected in his work as a spiritual impulse. His creative endeavors are infectious and can be found in numerous private and public installations around the world. His Miami gallery is situated in the very heart of the trendy Wynwood neighborhood. The studio is his free space to express and be realized, to once again create magic, to indulge the viewer into finding an independent point of reference.

Tunney has found aesthetic bliss. He is filled with high hopes and bursts with an incredible amount of energy. If you visit his studio, you can often just find him cycling around. He is every bit as inspiring as the refreshing phrases from his billboards that are placed in parts of the US and Canada. "I was driving into NYC, and every day, I'd see the same billboards. And it all felt so fake. The messages you're getting are drink, go to strip clubs, and take Prozac. I just want to put up a big billboard in Midtown that says, 'EVERYTHING IS OK.' Someone has to say that."

Throughout his work, Tunney evokes a positive attitude to life with slogans such as "BELIEVE," "COURAGE," "DON'T PANIC," "GRATTITUDE," and "CHANGE THE WAY YOU SEE EVERYTHING."

If you are wondering why "GRATTITUDE" is spelled with two T's, it's because in Tunney's world, gratitude is an attitude! And this goes all the way back to the time when he was riding his bicycle home from a tennis match and was hit by a car. He reflects about the incident with a clarity of mind that was not always available to him before he started to crank out art to fill his void: "There are no accidents in the universe. If you're in touch with gratitude, it almost doesn't matter what happens to you—because shit is going to happen to you—it's how you respond to it. If you're grateful, then I think you've got everything."

Old School Macro

This year marks the fiftieth anniversary of my father's career. If you were to remind him, however, he probably wouldn't realize it. He's not one to keep count. He's probably never had the time to look back and reflect, either, because I've only ever seen him press forward. His journey began out of necessity at the youthful age of fourteen, when most boys are busy playing sports or chasing after girls. He had time for neither.

My sweet old grandpa was an auditor in the army and only earned a meager sum. As the second eldest of eleven children, my father decided to give up his education to support the family. This was the first of many big decisions he would make in his life. He promptly left school and took up a training job with his maternal uncle to learn the basics of jewelry making.

He started working on his own when he turned eighteen, using just a few gold bracelets that my grandmother had given him, all together worth around $1,000 at the time, as start-up money. A few years later, he would leave Pakistan for the United Arab Emirates (UAE). He wanted to make an honest living, and achieving that in Pakistan was becoming increasingly difficult because society was on the precipice of a multidecade moral decline.

During 1971, while Pakistan was being split into two, Saeed Jewelers began operations in the UAE. My father worked hard at establishing his new business and kept sending money home to fund the education of his five younger brothers and to pay for the weddings of his four sisters. Those remittances entered a secular bull market, and his parents were eventually able to move to a comfortable new home.

By the time my father turned thirty in 1979, he had already made his first million. This was despite having his net worth sliced in half during the 1973 oil crisis. He was a wholesaler of gold bullion at the time, and he had received a large amount of postdated checks as payment. He was also surprised to receive a call from his mother that his father's health had deteriorated suddenly. Instead of using the checks as a security deposit to repurchase gold (which he always did because he preferred not to speculate on the price), he rushed to Pakistan to be with his ailing father. Upon his arrival, the gold price doubled in reaction to the oil embargo put in place by the Arab oil exporters as a pained response to America's involvement in the Yom Kippur war.

He was only twenty-four, and this was his heaviest blow yet—coming at a time just as he was beginning to make his mark as an entrepreneur. But instead of mulling over what he could've or should've done, he was stoic about it. I was discovering this to be a consistent theme throughout his life. It should come as no surprise that he has been an important role model for me. We all find inspiration from the stories of others, and when that story is seen playing out at home, the impact can be that much more powerful.

Over the span of fifty years now, my father has dabbled in many ventures: jewelry, textiles, property, chemicals, commodity trading, agriculture, airlines, and movies, to name just a few. He has faced several serious setbacks and even had his fair share of spectacular failures; but in aggregate, he was extremely successful in compounding capital over the long term. He is the original global macro investor, an original thinker, the ultimate contrarian.

Allow me to highlight some of his "trades."

My father didn't have a university degree, but he had the vision to fly to a village in Italy to learn specific jewelry design techniques. He had traveled halfway around the world when most people in the region hadn't even thought of traveling to a neighboring country. In the 1970s, information flow into the Arab world was pretty slow. He soon discovered that the price of silver was 50% higher in Bahrain than it was in the UAE, and most traders were oblivious of this fact. He would fly to Bahrain biweekly (about a one-hour flight) to take advantage of this price differential. In our modern day world of high-frequency trading, this would be termed an "arbitrage." He rode this trend for two years and reaped substantial gains before others caught on.

During the fall of 1980, the Iran–Iraq war broke out. Large scores of people fled the country. The public was terrified. Land prices collapsed. Fighting the natural human tendency to panic during times of extreme uncertainty (the war would last eight years), my father bought land at cheap prices. His friends told him he was crazy for buying into an illiquid asset at the time, but they would be proven wrong. He would repeat this exercise only a decade later when the Gulf War threatened regional security.

I was born in 1984—basically, my dad received a long out-of-the-money call option.

In the 1990s, he invested in a garments factory in the UAE. He had some well-known international brand names that were his clients, so his order books were filled with medium-term quotas under trade agreements. However, he foresaw that he would not be able to compete once China became a member of the World Trade Organization. He swiftly sold out of the business while still keeping some of those international contracts in place, knowing he would be unable to exit once the agreements expired. He decided to cut his losses short.

As we entered the new millennium, Pakistan was still dealing with a major political change, and there was much ambiguity around what the future had in store. Meanwhile, America was about to strike Afghanistan, which only added to the macro complexity. My father began making plans to return to his homeland and fulfill his one dream. He saw the rising demand for food around the world and decided to purchase large tracts of farmland across the country. This was not only a prudent investment, but an emotional one as well.

My father is a man of nature, and he loves maintaining his beautiful garden. As he gently observes the earth explode into different colors, I've never seen him enjoy anything more. It connects him to God. He can't help but marvel at His creation. He has spent many mornings surveying the plants around our house and the flowers at his feet. The blossoming buds remind him of his youth. The trees remind him of his own roots. The scented plants retell his life's story. The thorns are evidence of all the sacrifices he has made. The fruits he plucks are the blessings of his family. The withering flowers are a testament to nothing ever being permanent. Everything is loaned to us—even this life.

My father imagined living in a farmhouse where he could raise cattle, produce crops, and build a botanical garden. The intent was not to erect a fortress of solitude but rather to create a little paradise on earth for his aging parents and extended family members. He also wanted to construct a civic center just beside it to serve the underprivileged. He is now living his dream. Meanwhile, his call to agriculture was terrific, even from a financial point of view, and the value of his farm holdings is already up thirty-fold.

I have often wondered about what set my father apart during those formative years. What was the reason behind his outstanding success?

For starters, he was born on July 25, 1949, a Leo, the lion. Leos are known to be quite an ambitious lot, with an overwhelming sense of duty and responsibility to those around them. They are extremely strong-willed and courageous. They know exactly what they want and how to go after it with all their might and heart. On the whole, they have the incredible fortitude to work hard toward long-range goals and to persevere through any major obstacles that come along the way. I'm not sure where I stand on astrology, but this seems like an apt description by my dear father. But I don't think his success can simply be explained away by a constellation of stars lining up in a certain way. I feel what set him apart was the content of his character. And unfortunately for me, this is not something that can be passed on smoothly through genes.

According to George Santayana, our character is an omen of our destiny, and the more integrity we have and keep, the simpler and nobler that destiny is likely to be. My father did not just spend his life toiling away at a financial goal; he busied himself forming ideals and bringing them to life. Even though he was very young, he had the resolve to take a stand when the circumstances demanded it. He had the ability to look into his deeper self and find a belief so powerful that "it would give to a straw the weight of a mountain, and to foxes the strength of lions," to borrow a verse from Iqbal. His experience of trial and suffering strengthened his soul and inspired his ambition. But what I think differentiated him the most was that he had the astonishing capacity to match his self-confidence with the humility required to understand and appreciate God's will.

He didn't demand success; he merely accepted it as an offering—if that was part of the Divine plan—for his pure intentions and sincere effort. He always made sure that he satisfied his end of the bargain. The rest he left up to the Heavens. In this manner, he was never disillusioned, and even the failures along the way seemed like a gift sent from above. He never licked his wounds, even after enduring fierce battles. He understood, as Rumi said, that the wound is the place where Light enters you.

He's a tough act to follow. But I still aim to be my father's most profitable trade.

> **He adopted a role called Being a Father so that his child would have something mythical and infinitely important: a Protector.**
> — Tom Wolfe

Zaynab

I had a dream two years ago.

I was standing in an open field that was clouded by the night. Feeling tense, I trembled silently in anticipation. It appeared I was waiting for some news, and I didn't know what to expect or how to even react. A female figure approached me with something wrapped in a white sheet resting on her arms. As she came closer, my vision blurred, and I realized my eyes had welled up with tears.

"Congratulations," she said. "It's a girl!"

I couldn't believe it.

Batting my eyelashes, the tears began streaming down as I took the baby in my arms. I could barely see her face I was crying so hard. It wasn't under my control. The torrent of tears were pearls of joy and a token of thanksgiving. Although I had kept my feelings hidden in my heart of hearts, I was longing for a baby girl.

I abruptly woke up and found myself sobbing profusely, my face wet with tears. The whole experience was completely surreal. I knew I had been crying in the dream, but I was astonished to be shedding tears in real life as well. I had never felt anything like it before.

The timing of the dream was strange because I was unmarried at the time. It was also unusual because the odds of a girl being born in the Mian household were strikingly low. I'm number three in a band of four brothers—no sisters. My wife has two older brothers—no sisters.

Both my older brothers have a son each—no girls. My wife's elder brother has two sons—no girls.

My mother was crying when I was born. The pain of having another boy was more than the labor she endured. And when my younger brother was born, I think she didn't see him for a full week. I really felt for my mom. I knew she desperately wanted a girl, and no matter what anyone says, boys will be boys, and we can't fill that void.

It is a known fact that a daughter is the beating of her mother's heart. They are deeply rooted in one another. As I came of age, my mind was also set on having a daughter, if God so willed. Verily, I wished for my dear mother to experience the joyfulness of seeing a baby girl growing up in our house.

And then, just this month (on the sixteenth of August), my wish was granted, and the dream I had two years ago came true. Zaynab left the comfort of her mother's womb and entered this complex world. She is no longer cooped up in the dark with her eyes closed.

Unlike the dream I had, however, there was no soul-stirring or sentimental outpouring when I held her for the first time. It was contrary to everything I was told. I experienced no knots in the stomach, no melting of the heart, no choking at the throat, and absolutely no tears. I felt blank. But what I lacked in emotion, my parents made up for in abundance with their tub of love.

When she was first born, Zaynab looked like a teenage mutant ninja turtle. Hardly something you'd want to take home and show off to your family and friends. My mother vehemently disagreed, but I wish I was exaggerating. In only a week though—as if she already wanted to rebel and prove me wrong—her face turned rosy with illumination. She filled the world with beauty.

Now, I can't seem to take my eyes off her. My favorite pastime is to just sit still and watch her sleep for hours. I must have planted a million kisses on her bite-sized cheeks without her knowing. I'm addicted to that baby smell.

In the brief spells that she's awake, her cat-like eyes wander around as she soaks up all her surroundings. It convinces me of what Lusseyran observed many years ago when he said, "I am certain that children always know more than they are able to tell, and that makes the big difference between them and adults, who, at best, know only a fraction of what they say. The reason is simply that children know everything with their whole beings, while we know it only with our heads."

Zaynab is an old Arabic name that translates into "a father's precious jewel" or "the one who glorifies a father." My wife named her, and now, she's worried I will love our daughter more. She forgets that the greatest thing a father can do for his daughter is to love her mother, to quote Elaine Dalton.

As a first-time parent, everything is new. Even the feeling like my heart is now running around inside someone else's body.

> *Fathers, be good to your daughters,*
> *Daughters will love like you do.*
> *Girls become lovers who turn into mothers,*
> *So mothers, be good to your daughters too.*
> — John Mayer

Musicology

In esoteric music terms, there is something known as the "Divine Sound," the primordial sound that was the cause of all manifestation.

In the Islamic tradition, it is called *Kun*—the Quranic reference cited as a symbol of God's creative power. When God decrees a matter (such as the creation of the cosmos), He only says to it: "Be! (*kun*)—and it is (*fayakun*)." In the Hindu and Buddhist tradition, it is signified by Om, the sacred spiritual incantation. In quantum physics, it is perhaps referred to as the string theory, which states that everything at a quantum level is in vibration. The implication here is that the Divine Sound is the universal vibration.

The iconic inventor Nikola Tesla said, "If you want to find the secrets of the universe, think in terms of energy, frequency and vibration." We think of sound as it falls on our ears, but sound is actually a frequency spectrum. The natural tuning frequency of the universe is 432 hz, which vibrates on the principles of the golden ratio that is found throughout nature.

All the traditional cultures, many ancient instruments, and old churches that still have those built-in organs were largely tuned to this frequency. The greatest musicians, such as Mozart and Verdi, based their music on this natural vibration. The profound positive effects of this tuning on our consciousness and also on the cellular level of our bodies have been widely acknowledged. Rudolph Steiner, who pioneered eurhythmy in the early twentieth-century believed that "music based on C=128hz (the C note in concert A=432 hz) will support humanity on its way towards spiritual freedom."

Yet something happened along the line. For thousands of years, all of our tuning standards were based on the natural musical pitch of the universe (432 hz). But from 1950 onwards, for reasons that remain unclear, music was tuned to 440 hz. Removed from the symmetry of sacred vibrations and overtones, this tuning frequency is unnatural and disharmonious with the natural resonance of nature.

The surprising revelation is that almost all of today's music is out of tune with nature. Our ears are not built for the kind of music we listen to today. This is important to note because the ear is a conductor to the heart, and the sounds we hear permeate our entire being.

The science and art of cymatics, a process for making sound waves visible, illustrates that when sound frequencies move through a particular medium, such as water, air, or sand, they directly alter the vibration of matter. This implies that subjecting ourselves to different frequencies alters our own vibrational state.

Music scholar Maria Renold studied the different effects of vibrations on listeners created by 432 hz and 440 hz tuning. Over the course of twenty years, she asked thousands of people in various countries to evaluate how they felt listening to each frequency. Her results showed that 90% preferred the 432 hz tuning. When asked to describe it, they used words such as "completed, correct, and peaceful." Conversely, they described the 440 hz tuning as sounding "uncomfortable, oppressive, [and] narrow-minded."

Music is a subtle, suggestive medium of communication that has the ability to affect the ways in which we think, feel, and behave. And in today's world, music is found everywhere—shops, restaurants, offices, gyms, our phones, cars, and homes. There is no way to escape it, and it is all out of tune.

We all know that unnatural and genetically modified food adversely affects the physical body, but what about the effects of unnatural music on the soul? We must cultivate the ability to filter out the "noise" and attune ourselves back to nature, to the universal vibration, and to start living from our natural frequency.

> *There's music in the sighing of a reed,*
> *There's music in the gushing of a rill,*
> *There's music in all things, if men had ears,*
> *Their earth is but an echo of the spheres.*
>
> — Lord Byron

The Elegant Universe

> *Sonder*
> n. The realization that each random passerby is living a life as vivid and complex as your own—populated with their own ambitions, friends, routines, worries and inherited craziness—an epic story that continues invisibly around you like an anthill sprawling deep underground, with elaborate passageways to thousands of other lives you'll never know existed, in which you might appear only once, as an extra sipping coffee in the background, as a blur of traffic passing on the highway, as a lighted window at dusk.

We grow up thinking the universe revolves around us. Who can blame us? From the moment we open our eyes, people start cooing over us. "Look how beautiful." "She's so special." Friends and family hanging in our immediate orbit fight with each other to hold us for just a few seconds.

A sneeze, a cough, or a stifled cry, and our poor parents drop everything and run to us in a heartbeat. We are their masters, wielding invincible power. We constantly keep them on edge, making sure they don't get enough sleep or leaving them with just enough guilt to make them doubt if they are doing a good job. But for all the trials and hardship we put them through, we give them plenty of love in return. We're not inconsiderate, at least not yet.

For the first six months, the world, as we know it, is only as big as our mother's embrace. We are always wrapped in her arms. It is only after we crawl out of the comfort of her bosom that we understand our place.

As we walk around to explore, we realize that there are restrictions to where we can go and to what things we can pick up and put in our mouth. We are not free to do as we please. But the real shocker is to discover that we share our parents' love with Pippen, the family dog. That's an enormous blow to our ego.

When we turn five and our mother tells us that we'll get a baby brother soon, we sense trouble. Our worst fears are confirmed when everyone seems excited, even though he looks like a smurf. Slowly, things begin to change around the house. We get kicked out of our parents' bed and are forced to sleep alone in the dark. We notice we have to cry louder and longer to get their attention. And we are scolded for biting our younger brother to see if he is actually real.

Our universe starts to crumble before our eyes. How can we not be at the center of every experience?

Once we move into our teenage years, life gets even more complicated. We're so full of it, so full of ourselves that we struggle to reconcile with other people's wants and desires. Our personal wants reign supreme. So when we don't get picked for the basketball team or don't get the girl of our dreams, our sense of entitlement is bruised.

There comes a point when we stop believing what we know about the universe and its movement. We all, in one form or another, search for a new meaning. We are told our life's purpose is waiting for us in the real world, at our places of work. So we morph into this high-tech race of cyborgs looking to leave an indelible mark on the universe—much like the message we carved on our classroom desk: "Jawad Was Here, 11/8/97."

Years go by. We lose ourselves in the din of time and routine, becoming ghosts in shells—warding off boredom by scrolling through emails, Facebook, and other social media platforms. Thanks to our damn phones jammed in our fists, we live increasingly virtual lives, too busy and absorbed in our tiny cocoons. All the while, there in the background, faint and out of focus, the elegant universe moves in ecstatic motion. Sonder.

Fortunately, we are not journeying in the universe but *with* the universe. "Whether we are aware of it or not, we are all in a silent conversation," writes Elif Shafak in *The Forty Rules of Love*, echoing the wisdom of Shams Tabriz. She goes on:

> Everything and everyone is interconnected through an invisible web of stories. Do no harm. Practice compassion. And do not gossip behind anyone's back—not even a seemingly innocent remark! The words that come out of our mouth do not vanish but are perpetually stored in infinite space, and they will come back to us in due time. One man's pain will hurt us all. One man's joy will make everyone smile.

It's poignant, humbling, and thought-provoking.

We are all engaged in a dance fully choreographed by God—our caring parents, that snarky Pippen, our annoying little brother who is actually better looking, the beautiful girl who broke our heart, the guy on the train who can't stop staring, the Starbucks employee who is always smiling, our old fart of a boss we're avoiding, the homeless man singing, that couple over there fighting, the wind that is blowing, the kids going to school in the morning, Salma Hayek, me writing here, and you.

The entire universe is one being. To quote Alan Watts, "Each one of us is a very delightful undulation of the energy of the whole universe. Only by our process of miseducation, we've been deprived of the knowledge of that fact."

When will we take notice?

> *Learn how to see. Realize that everything connects to everything else.*
> — Leonardo DaVinci

The Reader

A few weeks ago, I had the pleasure of hosting Omar—an old classmate from high school—for lunch at my house, along with his lovely wife and eighteen-month-old daughter, Jana. We weren't close growing up—he was cool, and I was not—but we still often found ourselves battling each other on opposing teams on the basketball court. He played like Jason Kidd, and watching him dance around us made me want to raise my game. We would eventually compete against other schools on the same team and win.

Like the cast of *The Wonder Years*, we all went our separate ways and lost touch after high school. We reconnected only a few years ago and have stayed in much closer contact ever since. As a good friend, he has encouraged my stray reflections, and we have spent many hours discussing various themes in life. I still feel we are on the same team.

Omar is someone who comes across as having spent his years folded between the pages of books. He consumes books like candy, which may be a reason why he is such a great conversationalist. I'm lost around him. When we met this time, he gifted me a copy of *Ficciones* by the Argentine writer Jorge Luis Borges. I finished the book in a day, but what I found far more interesting than the short stories was the personal note inscribed by Omar on the opening page.

> Dear Jawad,
>
> Gifting a book is undoubtedly one of the richer interactions in life. The book, once gifted, returns to the giver a sense of personal ownership over the words within it. The wait for a response from the

reader begins immediately, re-enacting the real author's wait for a decision from the publisher. It requires him to humble himself before the reader by sharing the book in the first place. Amazing that such an intellectual pursuit causes such teenage angst. Thankfully, I've come to see it differently. A well-stacked library or carefully selected bookshelf opens up to a lifetime of conversation with the greatest of men and ideas. Their distilled reflections sit in purgatory on the pages of those books, unable to move until someone unchains them with their intellect or heart. If everything is aligned, they find freedom in the streets, homes, classrooms, mosques, and battlefields of all time. If given due respect, books should be seen as our worldly inheritance from the most Merciful. A taste of paradise for the soul to savor, a reminder of the limitless joys a limited body with limited time can never hope for.

Your brother,
Omar

My taste for books developed late. But I soon discovered it to be an ideal means to arrive easily at what others have labored quite hard for. For those willing to take the journey, books lead to an adventure of the mind. As a frequent traveler, however, I can't help but wonder what's ultimately the point of accumulating all this knowledge. Where (or when) does the intellectual quest end? If the aim of life is self-development, then it is our responsibility to realize one's nature. But can we simply read books and expect to unveil all the mysteries of the universe, especially the ones hidden within?

I've come to believe no amount of reading can ever teach all the thoughts and philosophy that arise in the heart. A person may either read a thousand books, or he may just open his heart and see if he can touch the root of all wisdom. I want to move away from bookish knowledge—which reinforces the ego and may take you farther away from the Truth that originates from the heart—and arrive at an awareness level through inner learning, which makes explicit the innate powers of man. Perhaps, I naively feel what we achieve internally will begin to change our outer reality as well.

There are many types of people in this world, but there are two that stand out based on my observation. There are those who look at life through their minds, and there are others who look at life through their hearts. There is a vast difference between the two points, and I'm aware of my own tendencies to forego the mind and listen to the heart. I now let the depth of my heart lead and let the head follow. After all, to quote Milan Kundera, "when the heart speaks, the mind finds it indecent to object."

I still seek mastery over secular subjects but only if I can translate a portion of that knowledge into experience and action, not just for use as a means to impress someone. Knowledge is sanctified only when it is seen as coming from the Source and must be ratified by practical example; only thus can knowledge be the impulse for internal change, making our learning permanent. As Rumi said, "Knowledge that isn't from Him is a burden. Like a woman's makeup, it doesn't last."

Acquired knowledge may vanish because it is outside of us, only that which is within can we call our own.

*Enough of learning, my friend!
You read so many books to become
all knowledgeable,
But you never read your own self.
You rush to enter your mosques
and temples,
But you never entered your
own heart.
Every day you fight Satan,
But you never fight your own ego.
Bulleh Shah, you try grabbing
that which is in the sky,
But you never get hold of
what sits inside yourself.
Stop it all my friend…
Stop seeking all this knowledge!
It's all in One contained.*

— Bulleh Shah

The Return

Just three days after I arrived home from Lahore, I received a phone call that my grandmother had passed away. For some reason, I wasn't saddened by the news. My immediate reaction was not one of loss and sorrow.

I enjoyed a very special bond with my grandmother. Even though we lived apart, I would call every Friday to speak with her. There was the space of an entire generation between us, and we hardly had anything in common, yet conversation with her wasn't difficult. She was like an old car engine. You just had to get her to start.

I was attached to her from a young age and always looked forward to her visiting me, which was not frequent. As I grew older, I started traveling to Pakistan more often, and I would make it a point to spend time with her on each trip. I pressed her for stories about her life, particularly inquiring about my Dada Abu, with whom I didn't get to spend as much time. She revealed a secret about him some three years back that changed my life. For that, and all the love she gave me, I will always remember her with a prayer in my heart and a smile on my lips.

In her last few years of sickness and hardship, I felt as though her soul was being cleansed. She was getting ready to leave us. I had last seen her just two weeks before. Even though she was in a lot of pain, she took my hand as I said goodbye and, after months of silence, sang a beautiful hymn for her last time. Her death seemed like a birthday present for my grandfather. She died the same day he was born and was buried right next to him.

I haven't experienced real tragedy. So for a long time, I feared death. Not my own, but the death of people I loved. Just the thought of it would crush me inside. It was only recently that my attitude began to change: I discovered that we must always be ready to depart. This life is loaned to us. We can claim nothing as being truly ours, not even our final breath.

So what is it to cease breathing, implores Khalil Gibran in *The Prophet*, but to free the breath from its restless tides, that it may rise and expand and seek God unencumbered?

Friendliness with death does not lead one to disdain life. Instead, it is simply a quiet submission to the inevitable. It furnishes a sense of calm trust. After all, death is not really death; it is an invisibility cloak. How can you cease to exist when you can live an eternal life in the heart of others?

If we lead a life in which we are not remembered by our loved ones, then we actually haven't lived. We must see right to the end of life and make something of it in our living—not for ourselves but for everyone else. What we gain in this world is nothing. It is what we give that counts.

At the death of Ghazali, the great eleventh-century Sufi, a poem he had written in his illness was found beneath his head. In it are the following lines:

> *A bird I am: this body was my cage,*
> *But I have flown, leaving it as a token.*

2015

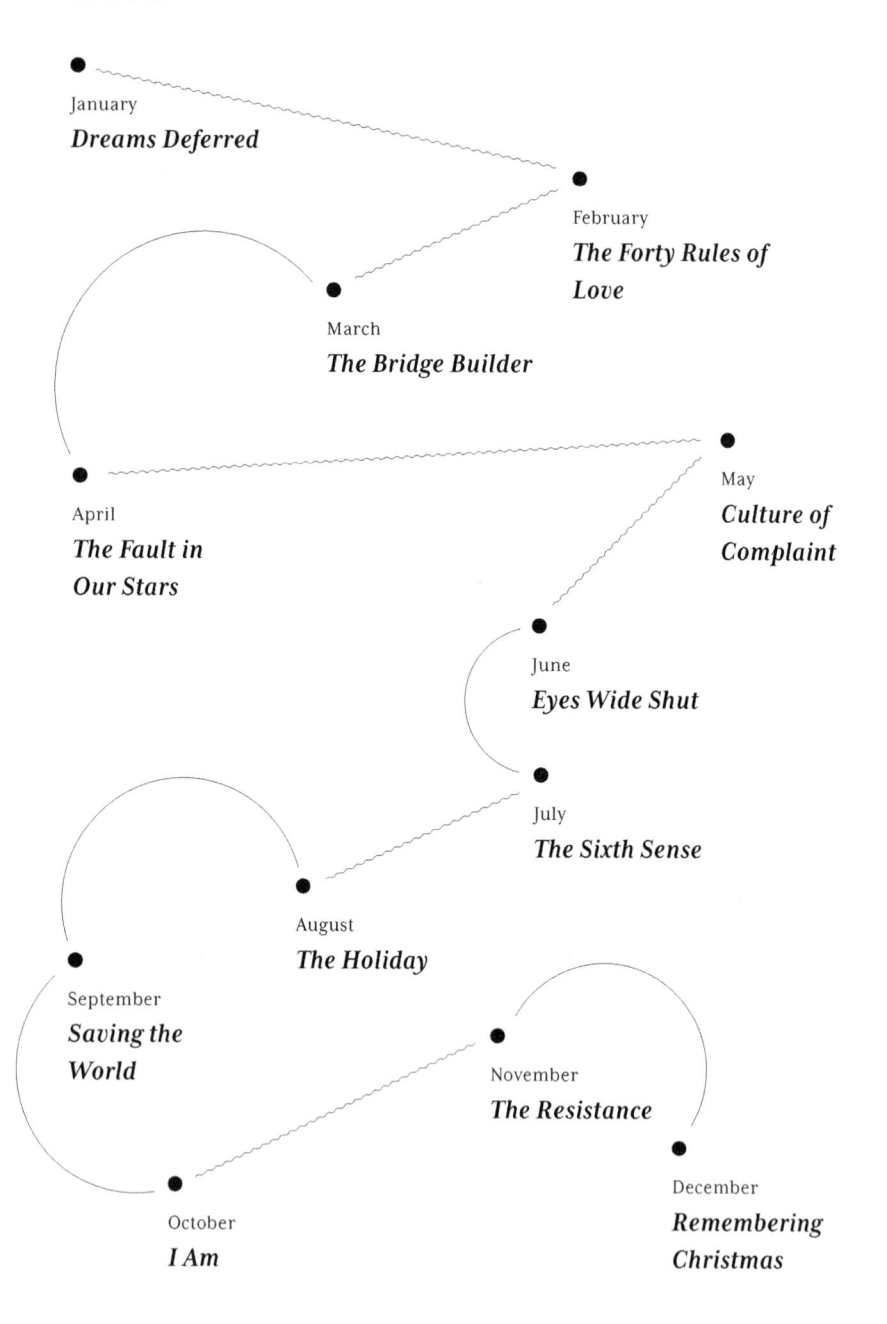

January
Dreams Deferred

February
The Forty Rules of Love

March
The Bridge Builder

April
The Fault in Our Stars

May
Culture of Complaint

June
Eyes Wide Shut

July
The Sixth Sense

August
The Holiday

September
Saving the World

October
I Am

November
The Resistance

December
Remembering Christmas

Dreams Deferred

> *What happens to a dream deferred?*
> *Does it dry up*
> *like a raisin in the sun?*
> *Or fester like a sore*
> *And then run?*
> *Does it stink like rotten meat?*
> *Or crust and sugar over*
> *like a syrupy sweet?*
> *Maybe it just sags*
> *like a heavy load.*
> *Or does it explode?*
> — Langston Hughes

Once upon a time, there was a prostitute called Maria.

That's the opening line from *Eleven Minutes*, an old novel by Paulo Coelho. I remember picking it up at the airport a few years ago and giving it a brisk read; I thought it was mediocre at best. My expectations were soiled because of my deep love for *The Alchemist*. I'm an incurable believer in the universe and its conspiring ways—that everything happens for a reason—and Coelho expressed that message beautifully through the journey of Santiago, the shepherd boy, in *The Alchemist*. As for *Eleven Minutes*, there was nothing about the book worth remembering, but for some odd reason, Maria had been on my mind lately. Last weekend, I flicked through the book again to discover why and noticed something I had previously highlighted:

She looked around her. People were walking along, heads down, hurrying off to work, to school, to the employment agency, to Rue de Berne, telling themselves: "I can wait a little longer. I have a dream, but there's no need to realize it today, besides, I need to earn some money." Of course, everyone spoke ill of her profession, but, basically, it was all a question of selling her time, like everyone else. Putting up with horrible people, like everyone else. Handing over her precious body and her precious soul in the name of a future that never arrived, like everyone else. Saying that she still didn't have enough, like everyone else. Waiting just a little bit longer, like everyone else. Waiting so that she could earn just a little bit more, postponing the realization of her dreams; she was too busy right now, she had a great opportunity ahead of her, loyal clients who were waiting for her, who could pay between three hundred and fifty and one thousand francs a session. And for the first time in her life, despite all the good things she could buy with the money she might earn—who knows, she might only have to work another year—she decided consciously, lucidly and deliberately to let an opportunity pass her by. She knew the time had come to stop. Not many people do.

I "stopped" four years ago. I'd been working at the "Crystal Shop" (for those of you familiar with *The Alchemist*) and decided that the time had come to follow my heart and intuition. It was a difficult choice to depart. After all, it has been well said that the three most harmful addictions are heroin, carbohydrates, and a monthly salary.

My father told me something when I reached out to him for blessings and advice:

> The natural instinct of a lion is to hunt for food. But consider what would happen if we take a lion out of the jungle and place him in a cage, and feed him regularly over a span of years—he would shed that instinct. If you then release him back into the jungle, the lion will run back to you and want to be caged again. The easy life creates in a lion the disposition of a sheep. The sharpness of his paws turn soft and become strengthless. The wakeful lion is lulled to slumber. Blunted are his teeth.
>
> We are the lions, Jawad. The lion is most handsome when looking for food. Tell me, why should we choose to stay in prison when the door is so wide open?

I was about to leave the security of success for an unknown journey no one knew anything about. Not even me. But I did not resist the changes that came my way and tried not to worry that my life was about to turn upside down. I kept telling myself, What if the side that is to come is better than the one I am used to? And even if it isn't, wouldn't it be worth at least discovering?

Life passes us by so quickly, and in my opinion, we spend too much of it planning and pretending, causing anger and resentment as we wait in vain. Instead of being farsighted enough to trust the end result, we turn fearful and lose faith. I knew that I needed more help than I can even possibly imagine to avoid running back in the cage, so I acquiesced to Grace. In the words of Rumi, "Doesn't the ocean take care of each wave till it gets to the shore?"

So to answer the opening question: I don't know what happens to a dream deferred, and I don't want to either.

> **We have two lives, and the second begins when we realize we only have one.**
>
> — Confucius

The Forty Rules of Love

> *I know you're tired but come, this is the way. Come, come, whoever you are! Wanderer, worshipper, lover of leaving. It doesn't matter. Ours is not a caravan of despair. Come, even if you have broken your vows a thousand times. Come, yet again, come, come!*
> — Rumi

Rumi is by far one of the most widely quoted poets in the world, yet he is also perhaps the most misunderstood. When Goethe, the greatest German literary figure of the modern era, became acquainted with Rumi's *Mathnavi* through German translations, he found it too complicated and difficult to comprehend because he initially failed to fathom the depths of Rumi's thought. Allama Iqbal had an identical experience, and in his early life, he mistakenly believed that Rumi was a heretic.

Rumi's relationship with Shams Tabriz, the thirteenth-century wandering Sufi dervish, has been the source of most of this confusion. Shams is credited as the spiritual mentor of Rumi and stormed into his life in the year 1244. Rumi was already a distinguished Muslim scholar at the time, but Shams would force him to unlearn everything he knew on the way to becoming one of the greatest and most passionate poets in world history. *The Forty Rules of Love* by Elif Shafak is a fascinating account of the inspirational relationship between them, exploring their quest for beatitude.

Shafak does a wonderful job outlining the Sufi spiritual path that lies at the heart of Islam. Take, for example, Rule 16: "Real faith is the one inside. The rest simply washes off. There is only one type of dirt that cannot be cleansed with pure water, and that is the stain of hatred and bigotry contaminating the soul." Rumi, it is observed through book, stood up for an inner-oriented jihad where the singular aim was to struggle against—and ultimately prevail over—one's ego, or *nafs*. He believed the undisciplined person doesn't wrong himself alone but sets fire to the whole world.

Here's one of my favorite passages from *The Forty Rules of Love*:

> This world was full of people obsessed with wealth, recognition, or power. The more signs of success they earned, the more they seemed to be in need of them. Greedy and covetous, they rendered worldly possessions their *qibla*, always looking in that direction, unaware of becoming the servants of the things they hungered after. That was a common pattern. It happened all the time. But it was rare, as rare as rubies, for a man who has already made his way up, a man who had plenty of gold, fame, and authority, to renounce his position all of a sudden one day and endanger his reputation for an inner journey, one that nobody could tell where or how it would end. Rumi was that rare ruby.

The Bridge Builder

I read a beautiful poem recently that helped me to appreciate the importance of illuminating the path ahead. The poem, *The Bridge Builder*, was written by Will Allen Dromgoole in 1900. He tells the story of a selfless, old man who stops to build a bridge after crossing a ravine. As the old man made the effort to cross the waters by himself and is about to complete his journey, an onlooker questions the purpose of his deed. The old man's response really resonated with me:

> An old man going a lone highway,
> Came at the evening, cold and gray,
> To a chasm, vast, and deep and wide,
> Through which was flowing a sullen tide.
> The old man crossed in the twilight dim,
> The sullen stream had no fear for him;
> But he turned, when safe on the other side,
> And built a bridge to span the tide.
> "Old man," said a fellow pilgrim, near,
> "You are wasting strength with building here;
> Your journey will end with the ending day,
> You never again will pass this way;
> You've crossed the chasm, deep and wide—
> Why build you this bridge at the evening tide?"
> The builder lifted his old gray head:
> "Good friend, in the path I have come," he said,
> "There followeth after me today,
> A youth, whose feet must pass this way.
> This chasm, that has been as naught to me,
> To that young man may a pitfall be.

He, too, must cross in the twilight dim;
Good friend, I am building this bridge for him!"

There are many ways to think about the poem. For me, it promotes the spirit of volunteerism, taking care of future generations, building bridges to help people and to guide those who will follow behind.

We all like to believe that we have made things happen for ourselves. But others have lit the path for us to follow. The footprints have already been cast. The path we take has already been trodden.

Once we recognize the contributions all the known and unknown people have made to get us *here*, we begin to grasp the design of life. It's not what we do for ourselves, but what we do for others that truly counts.

Build.

The Fault in Our Stars

> *The fault, dear Brutus, is not in our stars,*
> *But in ourselves, for we are underlings.*
> — William Shakespeare

This world is a *tamasha*, a grand show. In this hullabaloo, we all have our part to play. But what makes for a great performance?

Be in the moment.

The finest movie scenes are usually those where the actor is fully absorbed in the shot. He is not distracted with thoughts of the scene that he's just wrapped up or the one that comes next. The actor is lost in the current moment. We, on the other hand, rarely ever live the life that is right in front of us. Our days are spent extolling the virtues of our past or making future plans. Our happiness is not now. We either were or soon will be happy. We wait for it like a delivery from Amazon.

Shams, Rumi's spiritual mentor, guides us to a better life:

> The past is an interpretation. The future is on illusion. The world does not move through time as if it were a straight line, proceeding from the past to the future. Instead time moves through and within us, in endless spirals. If you want to experience eternal illumination, put the past and the future out of your mind and remain within the present moment.

Don't pretend.

As per two-time Oscar winner Glenda Jackson, "Acting is not about dressing up. Acting is about stripping bare." The most celebrated performances are the ones where the actor does not seem to be acting at all. The actor stays true to the character. It feels honest and real, even though it's all fake.

Instead of authentically acting out our parts, we usually just pretend. We make it up as we go along, leading a double life. We shroud our thoughts and intentions. Hypocrisy and deception become the norm. We get so deep in the habit of pretending before others that we forget our own character. Strangely, we appear disguised before ourselves.

Embrace uncertainty.

Great actors take risks, and they are not afraid to fail. They must face numerous rejections and disappointments before they are given an opportunity. Acting is a tough way to make a living. There is no stability or predictability in their earnings. This forces them to improvise, but it also gives them complete freedom.

We can't run from what's comfortable. Because we're so afraid of the unknown, we wish to have a clear-cut idea of how our story will unfold. We want to be in full control. Not knowing it is an illusion. So when things come at us from out of left field, we curse the universe.

Blogger Tim Hoch writes:

> It is little wonder that you believe the world revolves around you. After all, you have been

at the very center of every experience you have ever had. You are the star of your own movie. You wrote the script. You know how you want it to unfold. You even know how you want it to end. Unfortunately, you forgot to give your script to anyone else. Among the many shortcomings of your family and friends is the harsh reality that they cannot read your mind or anticipate your whims. As a result, people are unaware of the role they are supposed to play. Then, when they screw up their lines, or fail to fall in love with you or don't give you a promotion, your movie is ruined. Lose your script. Let someone else star once in a while. Welcome new characters. Embrace plot twists.

Soon the curtains will be drawn.

> *To live is the rarest thing in the world. Most people exist, that is all.*
> — Oscar Wilde

Culture of Complaint

Learn to lock up your tongue in the prison of your mouths.
— Al Tabarani

One finds cultures founded on guilt (typically in the Judeo-Christian world), cultures founded on submission (Islam), and cultures founded on shame (typicallyin Asia). Each is grounded in history and steeped in very distinct traditions. There exists another culture, one without borders that encompasses all. Taking people's stoicism captive, it seeps through everyday life and breeds disdain. Such is our culture of complaint.

With every morning, we ritually engage in perpetuating complaints— "I didn't get enough sleep," "The weather is horrible," "I hate doing the same thing over and over," or "I'm bored." Once evening sets, we make our way to the social abode of choice and talk obsessively about how the universe has wronged us in so many ways. There is much to complain about: life, politics, treasonous friends, and, of course, work!

On any given day, all these topics come up. This perversion of the mind lays hold upon us all. Individually and collectively, we engage in grumbling; daily, hourly. The many things in life we should be grateful for are lost in our worries and whines. Am I alone in detecting in people—myself included—an unappealing sense of ingratitude, the conceit of those blessed but whose heads swing in frustration because they fail to see their good fortune?

I often consider the life of the overworked underclass. They brave harsh realities and sustain their society, living austere lives of unrelieved scarcity. We protest: their fate is not ordained by God but by repeated bad policies and the self-interest of governing elites. Yet I encounter countless invisible souls who describe their own situation stolidly. They look up and give thanks for what they have and blame no one for what they lack. Perhaps complaining takes a listener and leisure, and they have neither. While we choose to drown in our sorrows, they simply get on with life.

Our misery and unhappiness, according to Rumi, is directly connected to our insolence and refusal to praise. Sadly, instead of thankfulness, we developed an ungrateful nature. Sa'adi strikes at our self-centered ego:

> The sun, the moon, the air, the water and the earth are all serving you, aiding life's purpose, and preparing for your food. Yet, you regard all this unthankfully, absorbed in your own little troubles, which are as nothing before the great forces of nature, always working, night and day.

When our tongue desires to complain, we should go contrary to it and find a reason to be thankful instead. For anything that could be better, there is always something else that could be worse. If we overcome our culture of complaint and get in touch with gratitude, it will change the way we see everything. The thought of the self will vanish, and the thought of others will take root. Rather than always wanting, we will care more about giving. Instead of relying on our imperfect understanding, we will look up to find greater meaning. Even virtues, such as tolerance and forgiveness, will arise in our hardened hearts as they soften. Life will thus unfold itself more beautifully. Our half-empty cup will fill to the brim.

So when I say, "I can't complain," you should understand what I truly mean: I choose not to.

Eyes Wide Shut

The story of Helen Keller is the story of the triumph of the human spirit. When she was only nineteen months old, Helen contracted a mysterious illness that left her without sight and hearing. She gradually adapted to her silent and dark world and forgot that it had ever been different. But as she aged, bitterness preyed on her. The desire to communicate and express herself eventually turned into desperate outbursts.

After being inspired by an account in Charles Dickens' *American Notes* of the successful education of a deaf and blind child, Helen's mother sought help for Helen. After months of effort, Helen's parents were given comfort by the Perkins School for the Blind in Boston that a teacher had been found for their daughter.

On March 3, 1887, three months before Helen's seventh birthday, twenty-year-old Anne Sullivan arrived at their Alabama home for the first time. For Helen, it was the most important day of her life. She was no longer without hope. Anne, who was visually impaired herself, became Helen's teacher and companion for the next forty-nine years.

Helen recounts this in her autobiography, *The Story of My Life*, telling of the many incidents from her early childhood:

> We walked down to the well-house, attracted by the fragrance of the honeysuckle with which it was covered. Someone was drawing water and my teacher placed my hand under the sprout. As the cool stream gushed over one hand, she spelled into the other the word 'water,' first slowly,

then rapidly. I stood still, my whole attention fixed upon the motions of her fingers. Suddenly I felt a misty consciousness, a thrill of returning thought; and somehow the mystery of language was revealed to me. I knew that 'w-a-t-e-r' meant the wonderful cool something that was flowing over my hand. That living word awakened my soul, gave it light, hope, joy, set it free! There were barriers still, it is true, but barriers that could in time be swept away. I left the well-house eager to learn. Everything had a name, and each name gave birth to a new thought. As we returned to the house, every object which I touched seemed to quiver with life. That was because I saw everything with the strange, new sight that had come to me.

From that fateful summer onwards, Helen rose above the physical and material conditions that surrounded her. With Anne's help, she became independent of physical sight and hearing. Helen describes this breakthrough experience:

Once I knew only darkness and stillness, my life was without past or future, I fretted and beat myself against the wall that shut me in, but a little word from the fingers of another fell into my hand that clutched at emptiness, and my heart leaped to the rapture of living. Now I rejoice in the consciousness that I can think, act and attain heaven.

Helen mastered braille and used it to learn German and French. She persisted in using her lips and voice, subsequently learning to speak.

She was admitted to Radcliffe College and became the first deaf-blind American to earn a bachelor's degree. She would go on to write twelve books and several articles on social issues. According to blogger Maria Popova, Helen blossomed from the inner captivity of a deaf-blind person to the intellectual height of a cultural luminary. Mark Twain, who had forged a unique intellectual relationship with her, wrote, "She is fellow to Caesar, Alexander, Napoleon, Homer, Shakespeare and the rest of the immortals. She will be as famous a thousand years from now as she is today."

Helen had cultivated a sense of kinship with the rest of the world and graciously embraced life. Everything around her breathed of love and joy and was full of meaning. She called this inherited capacity a "sort of sixth sense—a soul sense which sees, hears, feels, all in one." In her 1903 book, *Optimism*, Helen draws on her life and reflects on the universal quest for happiness:

> Certainly most of us regard happiness as the proper end of all earthly enterprise. The will to be happy animates alike the philosopher, the prince and the chimney-sweep. No matter how dull, or how mean, or how wise a man is, he feels that happiness is his indisputable right... Most people measure their happiness in terms of physical pleasure and material possession. Could they win some visible goal which they have set on the horizon, how happy they could be! Lacking this gift or that circumstance, they would be miserable. If happiness is to be so measured, I who cannot hear or see have every reason to sit in a corner with folded hands and

weep. If I am happy in spite of my deprivations, if my happiness is so deep that it is a faith, so thoughtful that it becomes a philosophy of life—if, in short, I am an optimist, my testimony to the creed of optimism is worth hearing... The best and most beautiful things in the world cannot be seen or even touched. They must be felt with the heart.

A happy life consists not in the absence, but in the mastery of hardships.

— Helen Keller

The Sixth Sense

> *Close both eyes, to see with the other eye.*
> — Rumi

In religious scriptures, we learn that God created man out of dust from the earth and then breathed into him His spirit. Thus, the body and soul are distinct, and it is the soul that gives the body its life. Isn't it strange that we pass through our whole life cleverly conscious of our physical body and yet generally unaware of our inner self?

From our early childhood, we begin to develop an awareness of our surroundings through the five physical senses—sight, hearing, taste, smell, and touch. This forms the basis of all our life experiences. But I feel there is more to human nature than what we live outward, what we experience on the surface. There is a tremendous power hidden within.

Inayat Khan speaks to this intuitive human faculty:

> We sometimes experience in life that which we see without eyes, hear without ears, and express without speech. It is the soul that sees, but we attribute sight and hearing to the eyes and ears. In absence of the soul, neither the body nor the mind can see. When a person is dead the eyes are there, but they cannot see; the ears are there, but they cannot hear. When the eyes are closed, do you think that the soul sees nothing? It sees. When the ears are closed, do you think that the soul hears nothing? It hears.

The ordinary senses are connected to our external organs: eyes, ears, tongue, nose, and hands. The soul connects through the heart, our most vital organ, which we neglect most of all. If only we knew what harm has been brought to it by our own thoughts, speech, and actions. The light of the soul only enters and illuminates the heart when the hardness that covers it is broken through.

The best practice one can make is to not let material comfort lull you into a spiritual sleep. The trick is to not starve your soul. This is very difficult in a world that is obsessed with feeding every desire of the body and seeking happiness through material pursuits.

According to Pascal Bruckner, our hedonism is not wholesome but is haunted by failure: "However well behaved we are, our bodies continue to betray us. Age leaves its mark, illness finds us one way or another, and pleasures have their way with us, following a rhythm that has nothing to do with our vigilance or our resolution." The moment we extricate ourselves from our exclusive preoccupation with the physical self and start nurturing our inner self—our soul—the latent power of the "sixth sense" will manifest into view.

Once the eye of the heart opens, a new consciousness is awakened. Our outlook changes, our insight deepens, and we develop a Divine point of view. We cultivate new ways of observation that bypass the ordinary senses, leading to greater unfoldment. This is beyond the understanding of the intellect, which distrusts thoughts that do not originate from the knowledge of the mind. And yet, it is these reflections, that spring from the depths of the unblemished heart of awakened souls that make explicit the innate powers of man. The whole world begins to seem different when this sixth sense awakens.

When will we, if ever, move from identifying with the body to identifying with the soul? Keep in mind that when we finally meet our death, the earth will reclaim our body; it is the soul that will rise and seek God unencumbered.

> *All day I think about it, then at night I say it. Where did I come from, and what am I supposed to be doing? I have no idea. My soul is from elsewhere, I'm sure of that, and I intend to end up there.*
>
> — Rumi

The Holiday

It is that time of the year when work slows down and those "out of office" replies surge as seemingly everyone goes on vacation. It is important to take a break from the humdrum of our daily routine—to reenergize and restore balance in our lives. Travel and change of place can do that.

But as I contemplate my own summer plans, I'm also reminded of Seneca's advice to Lucilius in the masterful book *Letters from a Stoic*: "If you really want to escape the things that harass you, what you're needing is not to be in a different place but to be a different person." Here's an excerpt of Seneca's sage words on travel as a cure for discontent:

> Do you suppose you alone have had this experience? Are you surprised, as if it were a novelty, that after such long travel and so many changes of scene you have not been able to shake off the gloom and heaviness of your mind? You need a change of soul rather than a change of climate. Though you may cross vast spaces of sea, and though, as our Vergil remarks, "Lands and cities are left astern, your faults will follow you whithersoever you travel." Socrates made the same remark to one who complained; he said, "Why do you wonder that globe-trotting does not help you, seeing that you always take yourself with you? The reason which set you wandering is ever at your heels." What

pleasure is there in seeing new lands? Or in surveying cities and spots of interest? All your bustle is useless. Do you ask why such flight does not help you? It is because you flee along with yourself. You must lay aside the burdens of the mind; until you do this, no place will satisfy you… That trouble once removed, all change of scene will become pleasant; though you may be driven to the uttermost ends of the earth, in whatever corner of a savage land you may find yourself, that place, however forbidding, will be to you a hospital abode. The person you are matters more than the place to which you go; for that reason we should not make the mind a bondsman to any one place. Live in this belief, "I am not born for any one corner of the universe, this whole world is my country."

That which we seek on our journey—to regain our sense of proportion and direction—is found everywhere, as long as we also make it a point to travel within.

Saving the World

> *I set out to search for wrong,*
> *I found no one wrong in the world.*
> *When I took a look at my own self,*
> *I found no one more wrong than me.*
> — Sultan Bahu

For a long time, my goal in life was to save the world. From what, exactly, it did not matter. There were countless causes to champion and multiple battlefronts to fight—poverty, hunger, corruption, hate, terrorism, health, human rights, environment, and education. Wherever you may happen to turn, there is always something you can find that is wrong with the world.

I joined groups, volunteered, made donations. But nothing I did was able to lift the weight placed on my heart. There was too much suffering, too much pain. Bursting out into tears made no difference. The human resolve laid deeply buried under the atrocities silently committed around the world. It was only when I opened myself to the indifference of the world that I began to appreciate the anguish in my own heart.

The truth—as I have come to learn—is that the world is as it has been and how it will be. It is only us that come and go. For centuries, we have not been able to rid ourselves of poverty or hunger, abuse or ignorance. What have we exactly achieved that we stand so proud of our progress and existence? Our track record is dreadful.

Take, for instance, the fact that the last 100 years have been the bloodiest in history. We also have more money and food today than ever before, yet our craving for worldly gratification knows no bounds. We have the collective ability to solve all of the world's problems but certainly not the willingness because we choose to hoard and spend aimlessly. It appears the biggest disease in the world is ourselves.

I'm left wondering whether my aim in life should be to "save the world" or to "save ourselves from the world." The world, with all its glitter, has been taken up so much in our thoughts that it has quietly taken control of the heart.

At some point in their life, everyone thinks of changing the world, but no one really thinks of changing themselves. Confucius believed, "To put the world right in order, we must first put the nation in order; to put the nation in order, we must first put the family in order; to put the family in order, we must first cultivate our personal life; we must first set our hearts right."

We are so enchanted by this world that we have made the world our heart. Yet shouldn't it be the other way around?

It is time to rescue our hearts.

> *Burn worldly love,*
> *Rub the ashes and make ink of it,*
> *Make the heart the pen,*
> *The intellect the writer,*
> *Write that which has no end or limit.*
> — Guru Nanak

I Am

> *We are all just a car crash,*
> *a diagnosis,*
> *an unexpected phone call,*
> *a newfound love,*
> *or a broken heart away*
> *from becoming a completely different person.*
> *How beautifully fragile are we*
> *that so many things*
> *can take but a moment*
> *to alter who we are*
> *forever?*
> — Samuel Decker Thompson

Tom Shadyac seemed to have it all—a multimillion-dollar career directing films like *Ace Ventura*, *The Nutty Professor*, and *Bruce Almighty*, a 17,000-square-foot art-filled mansion, fancy cars, invitations to extravagant parties, and friendships with other famous people. It was a life many people today dream about because it matches our modern culture's definition of success and achievement.

Tom had everything that he was taught was a measure of "the good life," yet he was not happy. There was a nagging feeling of emptiness inside. Then, in 2007, Tom was gripped by a crippling form of postconcussion syndrome after a serious bicycle accident. This was life-changing.

"Facing death can be a powerful motivator," he later explained. "I began to wake up to principles… I saw through the veil." Already disillusioned with the way society was organized, Tom sought to reorient and simplify his life. And he felt compelled to share his journey from crisis to contentment in an engaging and intellectually challenging documentary film called *I Am*. Tom attempts to answer the two big questions that inhabited him: What's wrong with our world? And what can we do to make it better?

As he sets out with renewed vigor to identify the underlying cause of the world's ills, he explores the work of scientists and the eternal wisdom of the great poets, saints, and philosophers. He also interviews eminent thinkers and writers of the day, from Desmond Tutu to Noam Chomsky. His findings challenge our preconceptions about human behavior and what we have widely accepted as the "truth."

First, it has been scientifically proven that the entire human race is connected. The string theory and quantum entanglement shows that this has more to do with the design of the universe than the simple fact that we are all humans. We are all wired to be compassionate; thus, some of the key sources of deep contentment are having many positive relationships, doing random acts of kindness, and serving others.

Second, society is at fault for training us from an early age to be goal-driven instead of values-driven. These goals separate us and make us feel competitive. And when we inevitably don't meet our goals, we feel sad, upset, angry, or tense. Actually, cooperation, rather than competition and "survival of the fittest," is nature's most fundamental operating principle. True human nature is to cooperate and unite.

Third, Tom learned that the heart, not the brain, may be our primary organ of intelligence and that human consciousness and emotions can actually affect the physical world. Yet we often denigrate the "emotional" heart for the "logical" and "rational" brain.

In a well-known *Hadith Qudsi*, God reveals, "I, who cannot fit into all the heavens and earth, fit in the heart of the sincere believer." In his poetry, Rumi implores God to open his heart in the way that He causes the rose to expand in full-blown beauty, not his brain. And Confucius says, "Wherever you go, go with all your heart."

Fourth, and most important, part of what's wrong with our world is that ours is a culture in which the pursuit of pleasure and the acquisition of "things" are seen as the ultimate measure of one's happiness. This violates a fundamental law that all of nature obeys and mankind breaks every day: nothing in nature takes more than it needs. And when something does, it becomes subject to this law and dies off.

Tom narrates in *I Am*: "A tree does not take all of the soil's nutrients, just what it needs to grow. A lion does not kill every gazelle, just one. We have a term for something in the body when it takes more than its share. We call it cancer."

The predicament of modern humanity, caught up in the quest for wealth and power with an ever-growing addiction to materialism, is that humans often take far more than they need by living excessively. Humans ignore the wisdom of St. Augustine, "Determine how much God has given you and take from it what you need; the remainder is needed by others." Or as Gandhi put it, "Live simply, so others may simply live."

Reflecting on his own awakening, Tom proclaims, "There's nothing wrong with making a lot of money. I was just taking in a lot more than I needed, and this wasn't good for me. I simply met myself at my needs."

At the end of *I Am*, Tom tells the story of when a newspaper invited essays on the topic, "What's Wrong with the World?" esteemed writer

G. K. Chesterton, often referred to as the prince of paradox, sent in the succinct response:

> Dear Sirs:
> I am.
> Sincerely Yours,
> G. K. Chesterton.

We all have the power to be what's right in the world.

> *If you want to awaken all of humanity, then awaken all of yourself. If you want to eliminate the suffering in the world, then eliminate all that is dark and negative in yourself. Truly, the greatest gift you have to give is that of your own self-transformation.*
>
> — Lao Tzu

The Resistance

> *Most of us have two lives. The life we live, and the unlived life within us. Between the two stands Resistance. It prevents us from achieving the life God intended when He endowed each of us with our own unique genius.*
> — Steven Pressfield

Everyone experiences Resistance. That negative, diabolical force of human nature that cannot be seen, touched, or heard—but it can be felt. It rises from within and aims to shove us away, distract us, prevent us from doing our work, to find out who we already are and to then become it.

We wake up with Resistance every morning. It has its own agenda and will do everything it can to keep us bound to it instead of actualizing our true Self. The clash is epic—between Resistance, which inclines us to self-sabotage, and the Self, which is trying to guide us from Divine ground—and the stakes are our lives.

Resistance is most commonly elicited in the pursuit of any calling in writing or the creative arts, the launching of a new entrepreneurial venture, any diet or health regimen, spiritual advancement, any act of political or moral courage, breaking an unwholesome habit or changing ourselves for the better, and, of course, the undertaking of any enterprise or endeavor whose aim is to help others.

In his book, *The War of Art*, Steven Pressfield delivers a battle plan to recognize and overcome Resistance. "The pursuit of art, originality, selflessness or excellence in any ethical form is, beyond all its other aspects, a discipline of the soul. It's a practice. A means to and method for self-transformation."

First, procrastination is the most common manifestation of Resistance. We don't tell ourselves, "I'm never going to start my own business." Instead we say, "I'm just going to start tomorrow."

Second, rationalization is Resistance's right-hand man. Its job is to keep us from feeling the shame we would feel if we truly faced what cowards we are for not doing our work. Resistance gets a big kick out of that.

Third, Resistance is experienced as fear. The more scared we are of a work or calling, the more sure we can be that we have to do it. Fear can never be overcome. So being paralyzed with fear is a good indicator. It shows us what we have to do.

Fourth, self-doubt can be an ally. This is because it serves as an indicator of aspiration. If we find ourselves asking, "Am I really a writer? Am I really an artist?" chances are good that we are. The counterfeit innovator is wildly self-confident. The real one is scared to death.

And fifth, if we find ourselves criticizing other people, we're probably doing it out of Resistance. Individuals who are realized in their own lives almost never criticize others. That is a sign more work needs to be done.

In the Quran, it states, "Not man as he is now, but man purified through obedience, self-dominion and detachment, can reach the highest station of Divine Viceregency," when he recognizes the potential of his innate powers, through action, instinct, and reason. But we must undergo long and painful travels to birth the perfect man or woman, which over time helps to acquire modesty and humility.

In Islam's Sufi tradition, the whole of their teaching is based on the crushing of the ego, or Resistance, which they term *nafs-kushi*, for therein lies all magnetism and power. As Rumi said, "Anyone in whom the troublemaking self has died, sun and cloud obey."

In the Jewish tradition, *yetzer hara* is what you would call Resistance. The great Kabbalistic teachers identified it as a self-contained and self-sustaining force whose sole aim is to block us from accessing the *neshama*, which is the source of all wisdom and goodness. That is why Rabbi Abraham Joshua Heschel said, "Life is lived on a spiritual battlefield." The war must be fought anew every day for as long we live. Resistance, which has its seat in the ego, cannot be reasoned with. It understands nothing but power.

Recently, I came across a definition of Hell that I quite liked: "The last day you have on earth, the person you are will meet the person you could have become." Let us strive to reduce the divide between that person and us. Work, struggle, endeavor.

Remembering Christmas

> *Teach us to value most eternal things,*
> *To find the happiness that giving brings,*
> *To know the peace of misty, distant hills,*
> *To know the joy that giving self fulfills,*
> *To realize anew this Christmas Day,*
> *The things we keep are those we give away.*
> — Marvin Davis Winsett

Shortly after I graduated from university, I landed a job as a bank teller in Toronto. It was surprisingly one of the best things that could have happened to me at the time. I was pretty shy growing up. I'm not a big talker. I was always the quiet one in our group of friends, and I probably still am. But as a bank teller, I was forced to interact with everyone—people of all ages and from various walks of life.

Slowly, I became comfortable in my role, and with time, I gained confidence. It was a small neighborhood branch, so it had a very sociable atmosphere. The branch manager (Vicky) was Italian, the two personal bankers (Nitee and Nydia) were Indian and Spanish, respectively, the financial advisor (Akis) was Greek, and my two sidekicks at the till were Irish (Julian) and Canadian (Kathy). I was there for three months and absolutely loved it.

What I remember most fondly from my experience was the period leading up to Christmas. I can't stand the cold. Even after having spent nearly a quarter of my life in Canada, I never got used to the winters there. But for some reason, during each Christmas season, I wouldn't mind freezing. I think it had much to do with the wonderful holiday spirit.

It was fascinating for me to see the entire city come alive. Trees and malls would be decorated with lovely looking lights long before snowfall had any chance to cover them in its fold. From November onwards, you could shop till you drop with big discounts at every store. And every morning, as I picked up my "double double" from Tim Hortons, I would smile at the sight of Santa and his reindeers doing the rounds on my coffee cup.

At our branch, the local radio station was always on as background score. In December, all they played were Christmas jingles. For the first few days, I went mad listening to the same lyrics over and over, but as time went on, I found myself humming along. My favorite was Chris Rea's "Driving home for Christmas," and The Pogues and Kirsty MacColl's "Fairytale of New York." I noticed our customers become friendlier as well. The grumpy old man was not so grumpy anymore, and the hurried small business owner found the time to say hello first. As Charles Dickens once observed:

> I have always thought of Christmas time, when it has come round, as a good time; a kind, forgiving, charitable time; the only time I know of, in the long calendar of the year, when men and women seem consent to open their hearts freely, and to think of people below them as if they really were fellow passengers to the grave, and not another race of creatures bound on other journeys. I will honor Christmas in my heart, and try to keep it all the year.

If you're looking for gift ideas, take a suggestion from Ralph Waldo Emerson: "Rings and other jewels are not gifts, but apologies for gifts. The only true gift is a portion of thyself."

2016

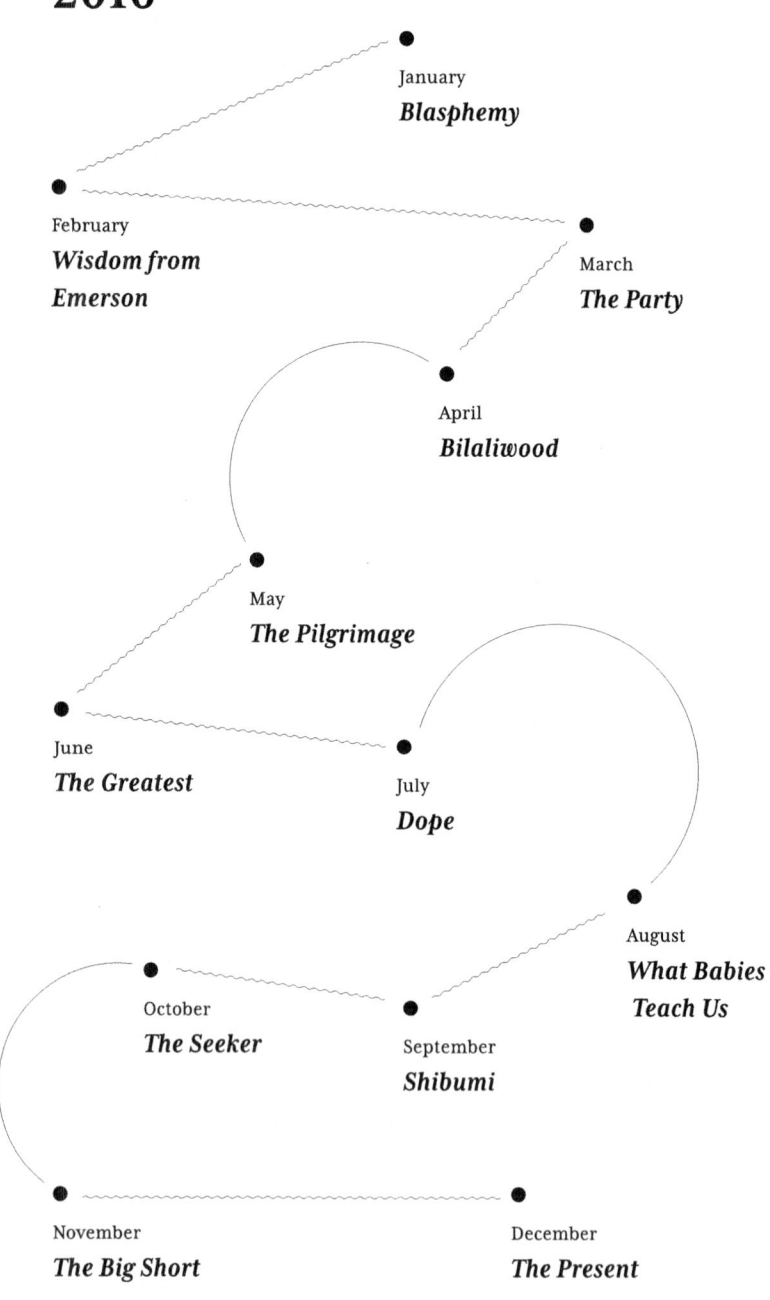

January
Blasphemy

February
Wisdom from Emerson

March
The Party

April
Bilaliwood

May
The Pilgrimage

June
The Greatest

July
Dope

August
What Babies Teach Us

September
Shibumi

October
The Seeker

November
The Big Short

December
The Present

Blasphemy

God is in a bear market.

Religious affiliation in the US is at its lowest point since it first started to be tracked in the 1930s per the General Social Survey (GSS) conducted by the prestigious National Opinion Research Center at the University of Chicago. One-fifth of the American public (and one-third of those between the ages of 18 and 30) do not belong to a religious group—more than double the number that was reported in 1990 and up significantly from 1972, when only 5% of those polled claimed no religious affiliation. According to author James Emery White, the single fastest growing religious group of our time is those who check the box next to the word "None." In the last five years alone, the "nones" have increased from just over 15% to 20% of all US adults. The unaffiliated, at 1.1 billion, has also become the third-largest religious group worldwide, behind Christians and Muslims.

The Pew Forum on Religion and Public Life has found evidence of a softening of religious commitment in the US public as a whole. One-third of US adults say they do not consider themselves a "religious person" and seldom or never attend religious services. The GSS also shows that the percentage of Americans who were raised without an affiliation has been rising gradually, from about 3% in the early 1970s to about 8% in the past decade. Based on research by sociologist Claude Fischer from the University of California Berkeley, Americans' level of religious involvement peaked in the 1950s. Nearly three-quarters of the public now seems to think religion is losing influence in American life, and most people who say religion's influence is waning see this as a bad thing.

If Ralph Waldo Emerson were alive today, he would surely be among those who disapproved of people losing their faith. He believed:

> What greater calamity can fall upon a nation, than the loss of worship? Then all things go to decay. Genius leaves the temple, to haunt the senate, or the market. Literature becomes frivolous. Science is cold. The eye of youth is not lighted by the hope of other worlds, and age is without honor. Society lives to trifles, and when men die, we do not mention them.

To be sure, the US still remains a highly religious country compared with most of the advanced world, both in faith and in practice. The Pew Research Center surveys find that the number of Americans who currently say religion is very important in their lives (58%) is little changed since 2007 (61%) and is far higher than in Britain (17%), France (13%), Germany (21%), or Spain (22%).

The rise of science and discoveries in new medicine has allowed God to take a backseat in our increasingly busy lives. We are living through an age defined by the cult of happiness, in which the "self" is the new god. French writer and philosopher Pascal Bruckner explains this as follows:

> On August 21, 1670, Jacques Bossuet, the bishop of Meaux and official preacher to the court of Louis XIV, pronounced the eulogy for Princess Henrietta of England ... The wonder of death, Bossuet exclaimed, citing Saint Anthony, was that "for the Christian, it does not put an end

to life but rather to the sins and perils to which life is exposed." The good death was a door opened on eternity, a passage to that "true, eternal life." In this life, by contrast, agony was expected. Is it possible to imagine an attitude toward happiness and living further from our own? The eighteenth-century saw the rise of new techniques that improved agricultural production; it also saw new medicines. Suddenly, this world was no longer condemned to be a vale of tears; man now had the power to reduce hunger, ameliorate illness, and better master his future. People stopped listening to those who justified suffering as the will of God. If I could relieve pain simply by ingesting some substance, there was no need to have recourse to prayer to feel better. In the 1960s, two major shifts transformed the right to happiness into the duty of happiness. The first was a shift in the nature of capitalism. Working no longer sufficed; buying was also necessary for the industrial machine to run at full capacity. To make this shift possible, an ingenious invention had appeared not long before, first in America in the 1930s and then in Europe in the 1950s: credit. Credit changed everything; frustration became intolerable and satisfaction normal; to do without seemed absurd. The second shift was the rise of individualism. Since nothing opposed our fulfilment any longer—neither church nor party nor social class—we became solely responsible for what happened to us. Happiness is no longer a matter of chance or a heavenly gift, an amazing grace that blesses our monotonous days. We now owe it to ourselves to be happy, and we are expected to display our happiness far and wide. Thus happiness becomes not only the biggest industry of the age but also a new moral order. We now find ourselves guilty of not being well, a failing for which we must answer to everyone and to our own consciences. To enjoy was once forbidden; from now on, it's obligatory.

Whether we like it or not, religion is still hugely influential worldwide. More than eight in ten people claim to identify with a religious group. The belief in a deity has shaped the identity and values of people and communities at every stage of the humanity's evolution. And yet, we can't ignore the fact that religion has also been used to promote controversy, violence, and hatred throughout much of recorded history. For whatever reason, our world today is increasingly fractured along religious lines. In our highly charged societies, religion cuts more deeply, arousing such powerful sentiments among people from different backgrounds that we are unable to put aside our differences. The whole world is fighting and destroying itself just because it cannot embrace diverse religious interpretations in an honest and calm way.

According to the Pew Research Center's latest annual study on the global restrictions on religion, nearly three-quarters of the world's population are grappling with high levels of religious hostilities within their borders. This is up from 52% in 2011 and 45% in 2007. Christians and Muslims— who together make up more than half of the global population— faced harassment in the largest number of countries. Harassment against Jews also reached a seven year high. Some of the countries in this category include Israel, India, Pakistan, Nigeria, and Russia. The share of countries where religious restrictions of some kind (related to either government or social groups) are either high or very high has also been rising. The tumultuous Middle East—where Christianity, Judaism, and Islam originated—still leads the world, housing some of the highest levels of restrictions on religion. China tops the list. Europe's median score on Pew's Social Hostilities Index (2.3) is also well above the global median (1.6). The harassment of Jews and Muslims is particularly widespread in Europe. Based on the study, Jews and Muslims have experienced harassment in thirty-four and thirty-two of the region's forty-five countries, respectively, a higher share than in any other region.

We, with our narrowness of mind and faith, agnostic or believers, have erected barricades of race and creed. What we really need is to break down these walls of falsehood so that we can once again strive to learn to live in harmony with each culture. Just as language has its own word for "mother," it is only natural that each culture has its own word to refer to the One who can't be defined—God, Elohim, Allah, Ik Onkar, Jah, Khuda, and many more words have all been used to mean exactly the same. For how long will we continue to make a graveyard of the globe?

Come, let us all be friends for once,
Let us make life easy on us,
Let us be lovers and loved ones,
The earth shall be left to no one.

— Yunus Emre

Wisdom from Emerson

Emerson and I are old friends.

I first discovered him during the summer of 2009 when I took an indefinite break to connect with myself, those little lulls in life that serve as nice, recuperative periods. Over the subsequent years, I have found plenty of answers in Emerson's essays.

Emerson devoted his young adulthood to studying Christian theology and trained to be a Unitarian Minister at the Harvard Divinity School. It was the same path his forefathers had trod ever since the seventeenth-century. On January 11, 1829, he was ordained to serve as the junior pastor at Boston's Second Church.

Emerson didn't last long. The great American writer had a very strong Christian faith but found himself in disagreement with some of the church's methods and general practices at the time. He made the following journal entry in 1832: "I have sometimes thought that, in order to be a good minister, it was necessary to leave the ministry. The profession is antiquated. I like the silent church before the service begins, better than any preaching."

Emerson was particularly disturbed by his first experience of slavery a few years earlier. On a visit to St. Augustine in Florida, he attended a meeting of the Bible Society while a slave auction was taking place in the adjoining yard outside. In the journal that he kept during his stay, Emerson wrote, "One ear therefore heard the glad tidings of great joy, while the other was regaled with 'Going, gentlemen, going!'" He couldn't reconcile racial discrimination and slavery with Christian teachings.

Emerson fought for change his whole life. He was staunchly opposed to slavery and believed in the immediate emancipation of the slaves. At the end of January in 1862, he gave a public lecture at the Smithsonian in Washington, DC, where he declared: "The South calls slavery an institution. I call it destitution. Emancipation is the demand of civilization. I think we must get rid of slavery, or we must get rid of freedom."

Emerson's social and religious views were often considered radical at the time. He felt the countervailing pressures of society had broken the relationship between the soul and surrounding world. He believed the presence of God is not to be found only in heaven, but also here on earth. For Emerson, the Divine was present and accessible in all things, especially in nature and in the heart of one's fellowman.

It's a small wonder that Emerson's central doctrine was "the infinitude of the private man." He published his thoughts in a series of essays and would eventually travel across the country, giving as many as eighty lectures a year. His ground-breaking work greatly influenced the thinkers, writers, and poets who followed him, particularly Walt Whitman and Henry David Thoreau.

Emerson was a true global macro poet. He scoured the world for the best ideas and gladly opened himself to differentiating viewpoints. Throughout his life, he took a particular interest in the religious writings of the East. He was an earnest student of a wide variety of books on Eastern philosophy, religion, history, and poetry. He was deeply moved by "the sentiment of piety, which stoic and Chinese, Muslim and Hindu labor to awaken."

Sociologist Dr. Craig Considine of Rice University highlights Emerson's affection for Eastern philosophy:

On several different occasions, Emerson singled out the Bhagavat Gita, which to him was "an empire of thought" and "the voice of an old intelligence." Emerson, however, did not limit his non-Christian exploration to Hindu scripture. He also translated roughly 700 lines of Persian poetry, most of which was written by the Sufi poet Hafiz, whom he described as "one of the great writers." Emerson was not afraid of turning to Muslims in the hope of gaining knowledge. His inquest into Islamic writings makes Emerson one of the leading American philosophers who encouraged his fellow citizens to understand others through reading and research. In his remarkable lecture "Religion" in 1836, Emerson even portrayed Confucius, the Chinese philosopher, as among a class of heroes who pursued virtue rather than worldly riches. He showed his appreciation for other religious traditions by stating that there have been noble saints "among the Buddhist, the Muslim, the highest stoic of Athens, the purest and wisest Christian." He added that if these saints could meet somewhere and converse, they would all find themselves of one religion, which reminds us of Emerson's belief in the oneness of humanity.

Emerson believed that all religions have great value and are thus more similar than not. Yet even during his time, Emerson felt that "we are now so far from the road to truth, that religious teachers dispute and hate each other." I wonder what he would he think if he saw the world in its present condition.

What we need now more than ever is for people to embrace Emerson's thoughts on religious tolerance and spiritual understanding. Unless we change, things will not change; and the disharmony of the world—caused by the ever-growing chasm between the West and the East—will only become that much worse.

To be yourself in a world that is constantly trying to make you something else is the greatest accomplishment.

— Ralph Waldo Emerson

The Party

Hafiz, whose given name was Shams-ud-din Muhammed, was one of the most beloved poets of the Persian language. He was born in the fourteenth-century and lived in the beautiful garden city of Shiraz. His work became known to the West largely through the intellectual passion of Goethe, the most esteemed German writer to have ever lived. Goethe's *West-Eastern Divan* was inspired by the mystic poetry of Hafiz and contained an entire section called "The Book of Hafiz." Goethe claimed, "Hafiz has no peer" and that he is "mystically pure."

Hafiz became a life-long companion for Emerson and deeply influenced his literary career. Emerson wrote, "Hafiz is not to be scared by a name, or a religion. He fears nothing. He sees too far, he sees throughout; such is the only man I wish to see or be. Hafiz is a poet for poets." The mission of Hafiz's poetry was to express to a fanatical religious world that all things are connected to God, meaning all things are Divine. He spoke of love, humility, and the importance of taking care of the soul through good action.

> *If God invited you to a party*
> *And said,*
> *"Everyone in the ballroom tonight,*
> *Will be my special Guest,"*
> *How would you treat them,*
> *When you arrived?*
> *Indeed, indeed!*
> *And Hafiz knows,*
> *There is no one in this world,*
> *Who is not upon,*
> *His jeweled dance floor.*

Bilaliwood

I'm not good with long-distance relationships. That's why, when I left Dubai in 2001 to attend university in Canada, I lost touch with my closest high school friends. We all went our separate ways—Badi was in Pennsylvania; Bilal in Atlanta; Naveed in London; Arhum in Illinois; Benny and Abbas in California; and Fahad in Ontario. Fahad was less than two hours away from me, but we only met twice in four years.

Although most of our group stayed in contact, I didn't. I struggled. We were all experiencing new things, and I just couldn't keep up over the phone or the Internet; it required too much effort. It also felt impersonal. After all, for the last five years, I had spent forty hours a week—just in school—doing everything with them.

And then Rehan, whom I met during my first week at university, introduced me to the "two-minute rule." "Dude, you can't talk to a *guy* on the phone for more than two minutes. It's against the rule," he said and hung up. It may have been our first conversation, but I was over my time limit. Hence, after this startling incident, how was I supposed to tell anyone my life's stories in two minutes?

Well, the truth is much different. And this truth comes to us from the poet Robert Southey: "No distance of place or lapse of time can lessen the friendship of those who are thoroughly persuaded of each other's worth."

I think I felt that, deep down, the bond we built in our wonder years would last us a lifetime. Even though we were all busy finding our own place in this crazy world, nothing could ever change so much to the point where we would forget about each other. No matter where life takes us, we could meet again after many years, freed from our contexts, and start over from exactly where we left off.

In his lessons on friendship, Aristotle claimed that friends hold a mirror up to each other, through which they can see each other in ways that would not otherwise be accessible to them; and it's this "mirroring" that helps them improve themselves as people. This is especially true of old friends who have known each other from a time long before we all wear our *masks*, trying to conceal our true selves from the world. The splendor of old friendships is that we don't give two pence about anyone's profession, status, income, religion, or previous history. Each man is simply what he is, and that's the beauty of it: we don't have to pretend.

On the way back from a speaking event in West Michigan last month, I decided to visit New York and spend the weekend with Bilal. I hadn't seen him in over a year. To my pleasant surprise, Arhum was flying in for work the same weekend, so we all crashed together.

Bilal is one of the best-looking men I know. He could keep a beard, shave his eyebrows, or tattoo the left side of his face like Mike Tyson, and he would still look dashing. He was the Hugh Grant of our high school, with his middle-parted hair and sweet English accent. It was not enough that most the girls in our class liked him. Even the teachers had a crush on him. Madame Hussein, our voluptuous French teacher, would make *purring* sounds as she approached the side of his desk.

Bilal has brains too. He was always one of the smartest kids in our class. He ended up going to Georgia Tech, where he studied biomedical engineering. He got into a PhD program that he later ditched to pursue a finance masters at the University of Chicago. Don't ask him why. The truth is, as I hold up the "mirror," I realize that Bilal is amazing at anything he puts his mind to. And right now, his beautiful mind is totally into music, which has essentially set his mind free.

Bilal is now a stockbroker by day, and by night, he turns into "Bilaliwood." One of his crowning moments so far has been playing the opening set at one of the biggest parties at Burning Man. He lives with his LP records in Brooklyn—just one block away from the awesome Ample Hills Creamery, which was the first stop we made after Bilal picked me up from the airport. Aside from having twelve scoops of "Salted Crack Caramel," what else did we do that weekend?

We just spent our time being stupid. According to Ralph Waldo Emerson, one of the blessings of old friends is that you can afford to be stupid with them.

The Pilgrimage

> *"What's the world's greatest lie?" the boy asked, completely surprised. "It's this: that at a certain point in our lives, we lose control of what's happening to us, and our lives become controlled by fate. That's the world's greatest lie."*
> — Paulo Coelho, The Alchemist

According to Paulo Coelho, we are all prisoners of our own personal history. At an early point in our life, everything is clear; everything is possible. We are filled with enthusiasm and not afraid to dream. But as the years go by, we simply let life proceed, without our noticing, in its own direction, toward its own fate. There comes a time when our personal calling is so deeply buried in our souls that it's invisible. But it's still there. In the silence of our hearts, it urges us to carry on.

Life is not without its challenges. If we do not find ourselves being trapped by circumstance, we are simply told that everything we want to do is impossible. We are so afraid of failure that we start believing in this notion and stop believing in ourselves. What we need is the courage to confront our own dreams: the courage to try, the courage to fail, the courage to succeed, and the courage to keep on going, even when the odds are stacked against us. To quote Rilke, "Perhaps all the dragons of our lives are princesses who are only waiting to see us once beautiful and brave."

As the thoughtful blogger Mark McGuinnes notes:

> These days, "ambition" is a dirty word. People who are "ambitious" are viewed as either selfish

or unrealistic. "That sounds a bit ambitious" is code for "you are going to fail." Yet, it wasn't always this way. We lost something important when we made a tacit agreement to keep quiet about our ambition. Because if you don't acknowledge your ambition—even to yourself—you risk choking it. You risk not only falling short of the best that you could do, but not even attempting it.

This bitterness can stay with us for the rest of our lives. "Twenty years from now you will be more disappointed by the things that you didn't do than by the ones you did," warned Mark Twain. So why not listen to our heart and follow the sage, old words of Rumi: "Let the beauty of what you love be what you do, there are a thousand ways to kneel and kiss the earth."

The universe conspires in favor of those who have set out on the path to achieve their dreams, even though we may not understand how. But to be worthy of a nod from fate, one must be willing to struggle. Not be paralyzed by fear. Naturally, we're afraid that in pursuing our passions, we may have to sacrifice what we've won. We are afraid of losing everything we have, whether it's the fame or the fortune. But this fear evaporates when we understand that our life stories and the history of the world were written by the same Hand. God has blessed us and taken care of us up until now. He's not going to suddenly stop showing up tomorrow. Faith for me has become a complete liberation. It drives away your fears.

Four years have passed since I resigned to unfold my own myth. At twenty-eight, I did not have the experience or the capital to set up my own fund, but I knew that there is nothing more crucial to investment success than the complete freedom to express my own views. The diabolical nature of the markets and the ever-increasing competition also meant that I must find my own answers. So I set upon a journey of self-discovery. I devoted myself to the pursuit of truth—in life and markets.

As far as I know, we will never be able to escape from our heart. If you are suffering at the hands of destiny, it is not unfair to ask God for a new one. He has no shortage of destinies for you. The great poet Allama Iqbal taught me an important lesson:

> Change yourself and your destiny will change with you. If you are dust you shall be scattered by the wind but if you become solid as a rock then you may break the glass. The world will shape itself according to your perception of it. Heaven and earth too will adjust.

Besides, in the end, it doesn't matter whether we win or lose. I just know this: when I leave this world for my scheduled meeting with God, I only want to be told one thing, "Well done, Mr. Mian. You tried your best."

The Greatest

Brash and boastful, Muhammad Ali riveted the world with his lightning-fast punches and fancy footwork. His tongue was just as quick, known for his poetic putdowns of opponents. He delivered blows with razor-sharp rhymes and comical one-liners.

In the run-up to the 1974 "Rumble in the Jungle" with George Foreman, the lyrical boxing icon told the press: "I done something new for this fight... I have wrestled with an alligator. I done tussled with a whale. I done handcuffed lightning; thrown thunder in jail. That's bad... Only last week, I murdered a rock, injured a stone, hospitalized a brick—I'm so mean I make medicine sick!"

A three-time world heavyweight champion, Ali left boxing for good in 1981 with a career record of fifty-six wins and five losses. What gave him the enduring strength and valor in the ring was that he didn't actually fight for himself. Money and personal glory didn't interest him. He prayed to God that he would win so he could use his name and popularity to help humanity.

"My fighting had a purpose," he told British talk show host Michael Parkinson. "I had to be successful in order to get people to listen to the things I had to say." This was all the more imperative because no one else had the nerve to say the things he did at the time when he did. A verbal dynamo, Ali stood unequivocally for truth. His firebrand speech made no exceptions. He didn't duck or run from anything, always ready to sacrifice everything. The courage of his convictions knew no bounds—and that's what made him "The Greatest."

Throughout his life, Ali was outspoken on race, religion, and war. He was a man of prodigious intelligence and eloquence. His words, "I ain't got no quarrel," served as a touchstone for America's bloody quagmire overseas and the domestic racial warfare that rocked the 1960s. Ali believed, "You don't really lose when you fight for what you believe in. You lose when you fail to fight for what you care about."

Even though Parkinson's disease silenced him early, his endearing charisma never left him. Ali kept up the good fight. He continued to travel the world to promote peace, to help fundraise for medical research, and to help support UNICEF, the Special Olympics, and many more charitable organizations. He always remained the people's champ and a "solider for humanity."

While people from across the globe poured in with love, thoughts, prayers, and support immediately upon receiving news of Muhammad Ali's passing, I knew that Ali himself had spent his entire life preparing for this moment. In a must-watch 1977 interview, when a young child in Newcastle asked him what he would do after he retired, Ali reflected on life and religion, finally saying, "Get ready to meet God." Muhammad Ali wasn't afraid of leaving this world. "My life begins when I leave here," he said.

I have spent the last many days reliving Ali's legacy—watching hours of his fights and interviews, reading his book and poetry collections, and tuning into his funeral procession and beautiful interfaith memorial service. It was an extremely moving and inspirational experience for me, as I'm sure it was for everyone who watched.

Toward the end of his book, *The Soul of a Butterfly*, Ali reflects on his life's journey:

There comes a time in every person's life when he has to choose the course his life will take. On my journey I have found that the path to self-discovery is the most liberating choice of all. There is a door to the heart of every man; it is either open or closed. When we value material things more than we value the well-being of mankind, the door to the heart is closed. When we are decent to others and share ourselves through kindness and compassion, the door to the heart is open. The greatest truth in life is that the happiness and peace of each can be reached only through the happiness and peace of all.

Change is an inevitable part of life. The seasons change, our feelings change, our appearance will change, and our health will change. Life is easier when we accept these changes and recognize how every moment of our journey is an important part of the growth of our soul. The man who views the world at fifty the same as he did when he was twenty has wasted thirty years of his life.

I would like to be remembered as a man who won the heavyweight title three times, who was humorous, and who treated everyone right. As a man who never looked down on those who looked up to him, and who helped as many people as he could. As a man who stood up for his beliefs no matter what. As a man who tried to unite all humankind through faith and love. And if all that's too much, then I guess I'd settle for being remembered only as a great boxer who became a leader and a champion of his people, and I wouldn't even mind if folks forgot how pretty I was.

A man's true greatness lies in the consciousness of an honest purpose in life, founded on a just estimate of himself and everything else, on frequent self-examinations, and a steady obedience to the rule which he knows to be right, without troubling himself about what others may think or say.

— Marcus Aurelius

Dope

Five years ago, I was technologically challenged. I didn't tweet or share pictures on Instagram, and you couldn't add me as your friend on Facebook. I was even the last among my family to download WhatsApp. I had heard of podcasts but never actually listened to one. I was cool enough to carry an iPhone but not savvy to have more than five apps on it. I liked keeping things simple, and this new wave of technology just seemed too complicated. But seeing it evolve as the biggest macro force and begin to invade all aspects of our life, I was forced to update my preferences.

Now, each morning begins with a full immersion in the stream of Internet consciousness. I reach for my phone first thing and check the overnight news, scan countless tweets, and respond to multiple emails—only then do I get out of bed.

This just sets the day off badly because all the "notifications" make me feel like I'm already behind. I am left catching up through the day and have a tough time getting any new work done. But it doesn't stop there. I take little dopamine snacks all day long. You don't know when a new tweet or an email may show up, so I manically check my phone all the time. I strangely enjoy this unpredictability and sense of surprise.

In the 1980s, Dr. Wolfram Schultz, a professor of neuroscience at Cambridge University, showed through a series of experiments on rats that dopamine relates to the reward we receive for an action. Receiving texts, hearts, likes, and thumbs-up has been shown to stimulate the dopamine system and light up the same area of the brain affected by addictive drugs and alcohol. This compulsive feedback loop—always plugged in, always checking, always updating—explains why it becomes harder and harder to take a break from our virtual living. Smartphones are a toxic fix for dopamine junkies.

Studies have shown people use their phones over four hours a day. Most of these interactions are for less than thirty seconds, but they add up. The average person will spend two years of their life on Facebook. People thumb 300 feet a day on their newsfeed, the height of the statue of liberty.

The Harvard Grant Study tracked 268 sophomore students for seventy-five years and looked at what factors made them more or less happy. The presence of one thing predicted unhappiness better than anything else: alcohol. It led to failed marriages, depression, careers coming off the rails, and bad health. In the coming years, might we see the same effects from the ubiquitous use of smartphones, which release the same neurochemicals? According to writer Andrew Sullivan, our enslavement to dopamine has simply made us less aware of our unhappiness, "our phones are merely new and powerful antidepressants of a nonpharmaceutical variety."

Close relationships, more than money or fame, are what keep people happy throughout their lives, which is something the Harvard study also revealed. Those ties protect people from life's discontents, help to delay mental and physical decline, and are better predictors of long and fulfilling lives than social class, IQ, or even genes. But people today are engrossed in virtual interactions rather than meaningful human encounters. Real-world connections are becoming onerous. And feeling socially isolated is common among youth. Even families live, what psychologist Sherry Turkle refers to as, "alone together."

One of the principles of mindfulness is the following: you are where your attention is. This means I am nowhere and everywhere at once. Being connected to technology has become surprisingly stressful, fostering an environment of almost constant interruptions and distractions. My writing has suffered as result. I find no time for silence and reflection, always being absorbed in some trivia online. The endless bombardment of news and information overwhelms me—and I don't even use Facebook or Instagram. I've stopped reading books as a result.

"Paying attention is the purest form of love," said Mother Theresa. What bothers me the most is that my daughter has to compete with my phone for my attention. My wife thinks that I'm never "present," and I don't blame her. I was smitten by my smartphone. But that's it—I'm done! I admit that I am powerless over my smartphone, that I have finally reached my limit. I am now going to rebalance my life—with more time spent in the physical world, being more aware, more conscious, and less in a virtual cloud. Like kicking any harmful addiction, though, this is going to require an enormous level of determination.

Here are some steps I'm planning: 1) don't cradle my phone before going to sleep, 2) don't check my phone until at least a couple of hours have passed in the morning, 3) place the phone in a different room from where I am and don't bring it into the bathroom at all, 4) keep the ringer silent and switch off all notifications, 5) stop the flow of emails by fetching them manually, 6) quit microblogging my thoughts, 7) restrict phone use to a maximum of twenty times a day, and 8) don't text and drive.

At various moments, I still find myself giving in, but I'm not giving up. I don't want to spend my life doped out.

What Babies Teach Us

> *While we try to teach our children all about life, our children teach us what life is all about.*
> — Angela Schwindt

Zaynab turns two years old this month. As a first-time father, I also turn two in my experience as a parent. I feel like we are growing up together.

For the last two years, I've watched Zaynab marvel at this world of sights and sounds in what was, without question, the most accelerated period of learning in her life—putting everything she can into her mouth as a way of connecting with it, pushing her explorations further as she learned to crawl, stand, and walk, establishing her individual identity as she distinguished between this thing called "Zaynab" (she refers to herself in third person) and everything else, and now, using the gift of speech to make sense of her surroundings and negotiate her existence in the world. She is absorbing new observations a mile a minute and developing an awareness of herself as an autonomous, self-determining being.

With all the hours of attention we give our children, we naturally think we are the ones teaching them. But if we dare to pay close enough attention, they have a host of important lessons for us, too.

One of my greatest joys is to watch my parents spend time with Zaynab. How she folds into their arms so neatly, how they shower her with endless warmth and affection. It allows me to imagine something that just never occurred to me before: thirty years ago, it was probably me they had in their arms; I was the one they were obsessing over. As a witness to their incredible outpouring of love for their granddaughter, I am humbled by how much love they must have felt for me. It makes me sad for ever raising my voice at my father in a heated argument. And it makes me appreciate my mother's sacrifices even more, which continue to this day. I should, perhaps, be more kind and say, "I love you" more often.

However different we may all be now, we were all babies once. It's easy to play it tough now, to overdo our independence, but we have all been recipients of continuous selfless and exhaustive attention, at all hours and in multiple ways. And therefore, no one made themselves; there is no "self-made" man. Babies are a reminder that we're dependent creatures. Today, they need us. Tomorrow, we will need them. Now, we hold their hand. Later, they will hold ours.

As adults, we struggle to make someone happy or even feel happy ourselves. But ostensibly, minor things please babies. Things that have become boring to us, perhaps unfairly so, excite them to no end. Zaynab encourages us to celebrate even the most ordinary experiences of life as precious Divine gifts. It's so easy for her to put a smile on someone's face.

Philosopher Alain de Botton believes we should hang out with babies as a corrective, to remind us of what really matters:

> It's easy to get sickened by our species: the greed, the status consciousness, the vanity. Babies don't care if the car is big, they don't pay attention to what one's job is or how much one's making. They teach us about the truest, purest, ego-free kind of love, which is about giving affection without

an expectation of receiving anything in return.

I find them to be the utmost spiritual teachers. No one is born hating another person because of the color of his skin, because of his background, or because of his religion. Babies only care about being with people who are nice to them, whatever they look like. From three months of age, research has found babies actually understand the difference between "mean" and "helpful" behavior and have a natural instinct to favor the latter.

Most of all, they're messengers of hope, a testament that no matter how much hate there is in the world, love will never be defeated. So much is this true that even faced with death and destruction, they have the power to prevent us from feeling too disenchanted with the state of our world.

> ***Once in the past,***
> ***I asked a bird***
> ***"In what way do you fly***
> ***In this gravity of wickedness?"***
> ***She responded,***
> ***"Love lifts my wings."***
>
> — Hafiz

Shibumi

One of the great joys of writing is that you connect with people from around the world, sparking an exchange that leads to newer discoveries. This happened with me on a recent trip to Sun Valley, Idaho.

I was invited to speak at a special private gathering and received an email out of the blue from Heidi, who found out I was going to be there. She lives in a resort town known for being a celebrity hideout, with its magnificent nature and spectacular winter scenery that serves as a place for inspiration for writers, actors, and poets. So we arranged to meet for breakfast.

"Your blog is my favorite read," said Heidi, as we sat down. I blushed, though you could not tell from my thick beard. It was the first time anyone had ever said that to me, and I didn't know how to react. I just felt honored being in her presence.

For the next two hours, I shared my life's journey, opening up to an extent that surprised me. I felt instantly comfortable around Heidi and was captivated by her calm energy. It was like we had known each other a long while. She listened intently and chimed in with stories from her own life. We spoke about everything—favorite books and travels, marriage and children, our work and passions, fears and weaknesses, everything, that is, except markets.

"Are you familiar with *shibumi*?" asked Heidi.

"No, what's that?"

"Well, *shibumi* is a Japanese word, but because their language is so rich in subtle nuances and the word is used so often, it has so many definitions that apparently people have given up trying to define it. It just *is*."

"What does it mean to you?"

"Shibumi is an ineffable quality, a place of overwhelming calm that we should seek to find."

I liked the sound of that. And realized Heidi's secret was her determination to attain a rare kind of personal excellence, a state of effortless perfection, known only as *shibumi*. She recommended reading *Shibumi*, a 1979 best-selling novel by Trevanian, nom de plume of Rodney William Whitaker, to learn more. Here's an excerpt:

> Shibumi has to do with great refinement underlying commonplace appearances. It is a statement so correct that it does not have to be bold, so poignant it does not have to be pretty, so true it does not have to be real. Shibumi is understanding, rather than knowledge. Eloquent silence. In demeanor, it is modesty without prudency. In art, where the spirit of shibumi takes the form of *sabi*, it is elegant simplicity. In philosophy, where shibumi emerges as *wabi*, it is spiritual tranquility that is not passive; it is being without the angst of becoming. And in the personality of a man, it is... how does one say it? Authority without domination? Something like that.

Nicholai's imagination was galvanized by the concept of shibumi. No other ideal had ever touched him so. "How does one achieve this shibumi, sir?"

"One does not achieve it, one... discovers it. And only a few men of infinite refinement ever do that. Men like my friend Otake-san."

"Meaning that one must learn a great deal to arrive at shibumi?"

"Meaning, rather, that one must pass through knowledge and arrive at simplicity."

With good intention and strong will, we can gradually, and above all graciously, bring *shibui* into our life.

The Seeker

What you seek is seeking you.
— Rumi

Written in 1922, *Siddhartha* is an allegorical novel by Hermann Hesse. It deals with the story of a restless Indian boy named Siddhartha, who leaves the comfort of his home and embarks upon a spiritual journey in search of peace and wisdom.

On his quest, he first spends time with the Samanas, who encourage him to live a life of deprivation. He practices fasting, meditation, and self-denial, but all his efforts are in vain. He feels no closer to enlightenment. He tells his friend, Govinda, who also accompanied him on the journey, of his doubts:

> I find only a short numbing of the senses in my exercises and meditations and that I am just as far removed from wisdom, from salvation, as a child in the mother's womb.

His unrelenting search for a universal understanding of life takes him to Gautama, the Buddha himself. He had heard that he was a man of bliss and that Brahmans and princes would bow down before him and become his students. He decides to walk over to the town of Savathi to meet the exalted one:

> He looked at Gautama's head, his shoulders, his feet, his quietly dangling hand, and it seemed to him as if every joint of every finger of this hand

> was of these teachings, spoke of, breathed of, exhaled the fragrant of, glistened of truth. This man, this Buddha was truthful down to the gesture of his last finger. This man was holy.

Never before had Siddhartha venerated a person so much, never before had he loved a person as much as this one. But Siddhartha felt little curiosity for his teachings; he did not believe that they would teach him anything new. He felt strongly that true wisdom can only come from within. So while Govinda chose to stay and sought refuge with the monks, Siddhartha moved on.

He ventures into the city where he meets Kamala, a courtesan who sends him in the direction of material pursuits. Even as a rich man, however, Siddhartha realizes that the luxurious lifestyle he has chosen is merely an illusion, empty of spiritual fulfillment:

> He had been captured by the world, by lust, covetousness, sloth, and finally also by that vice which he had used to despise and mock the most as the most foolish one of all vices: greed. Property, possessions, and riches also had finally captured him; they had become a shackle and a burden.

With a gloomy mind, Siddhartha leaves everything behind and decides to live the rest of his life by a river, where he had earlier met Vasudeva, an enlightened ferry man. He becomes an observer of nature, and the river teaches him many lessons, with Vasudeva as his guide. He learns from it continually. Above all, he learns to surrender. Siddhartha also realizes that he had learned something new from everyone he has met on his path. There is Truth all around. From that moment, Siddhartha ceases to fight against his destiny and thinks only of the Oneness of all life:

> There shone in his face the serenity of knowledge, of one who is no longer confronted with conflict of desires, who has found salvation, who is in harmony with the stream of events, with the stream of life, full of sympathy and compassion, surrendering himself to the stream, belonging to the unity of all things. He was an inspired man.

Years later, Govinda, still restless in his heart, comes to the river after hearing talk of an old ferryman who is regarded as wise. He asks Siddhartha to ferry him over, not recognizing him at first as the friend of his youth. As the two old friends begin their trip across the river, Govinda asks Siddhartha to share some of the things he learned on his journey:

> What could I say to you that would be of value, except that perhaps you seek too much, that as a result of your seeking you cannot find. When someone is seeking, it happens quite easily that he only sees the thing that he is seeking; that he is unable to find anything, unable to absorb anything, because he is only thinking of the thing he is seeking, because he has a goal, because he is obsessed with his goal. Seeking means: to have a goal; but finding means: to be free, to be receptive, to have no goal. You, O worthy one, are perhaps indeed a seeker, for in striving towards your goal, you do not see many things that are under your nose.

Don't we all spend our life searching for something? We write our goals, design our path, and then chase after it with everything that we have. We pursue our objectives aggressively and directly, ignoring all other possibilities, and we try our best not to deviate from the plan.

In place of hurrying on the path with our hands stretched out, reaching for the goal—which always seems farther away, fleeing from our grasp even as we think we are getting closer—perhaps we should walk through life with our arms wide open and our palms tilted toward the sky. In this manner, we would be open to receiving everything that comes our way, living in the present as opposed to in some uncertain future. Rather than feeling tired of life and the long road we still have to travel ahead, we would be free of worry and slowly discover the joy of surprising ourselves instead. Maybe we will learn something new on every step along the way.

When Siddhartha glanced at the river, he realized something: "This water ran and ran, incessantly it ran, and was nevertheless always there, was always at all times the same, and yet, new in every moment!"

I've grown up to believe there are no coincidences in life. We are always in the right place, and everything happens at exactly the right time. Instead of obsessing about our goals or destination, maybe we should remain in the present moment and just let the universe move about. Like the river, life has its own flow; we cannot impose our own structure on it. We can't control it—all we can do is listen to its current. Sometimes, when the outside noise dulls down, the quietness within reveals a lot, but only if you listen intently.

The Big Short

He that is down needs fear no fall,
He that is low, no pride;
He that is humble ever shall
Have God to be his guide.
I am content with what I have,
Little be it or much;
And, Lord, contentment still I crave
Because Thou savest such.
Fullness to such a burden is,
That go in pilgrimage;
Here little and hereafter bliss,
Is best from all to age.
— John Bunyan

I recently read and very much enjoyed *The Screwtape Letters* by C. S. Lewis. A masterpiece of religious satire, the story takes the form of a series of letters from Screwtape, a Senior Demon in the bureaucracy of Hell, that are sent to his novice nephew and protégé Wormwood, a Junior Tempter, who is charged with the responsibility of securing the damnation of an ordinary young man known only as "the Patient."

Screwtape schemes meticulously and instructs Wormwood on how to corrupt the patient and undermine his faith in various subtle ways, thereby encouraging him, little by little, to drift away from "the Enemy" (God) and toward exclusive preoccupation with this ephemeral world.

Take this timely advice for example:

My Dear Wormwood,

Be sure that the patient remains completely fixated on politics. Arguments, political gossip, and obsessing on the faults of people they have never met serves as an excellent distraction from advancing in personal virtue, character, and the things the patient can control. Make sure to keep the patient in a constant state of angst, frustration and general disdain towards the rest of the human race in order to avoid any kind of charity or inner peace from further developing. Ensure that the patient continues to believe that the problem is "out there" in the "broken system" rather than recognizing there is a problem with himself.

Keep up the good work,
Uncle Screwtape

Through this humorous and perceptive tale, C. S. Lewis delves into human nature and moral questions about good versus evil, temptation, repentance, and grace, leaving the reader with a better understanding of what it means to live a faith-centered life. Although the entire book is filled with incredible wit and wisdom, the following exchange resonated with me the most:

My Dear Wormwood,

The long, dull, monotonous years of middle-aged prosperity or middle-aged adversity are excellent campaigning weather. You see, it is so hard for these creatures to persevere. The routine of adversity, the gradual decay of youthful loves and youthful hopes, the quiet despair of ever overcoming the chronic temptations with which we have again and again defeated them, the drabness which we create in their lives and the inarticulate resentment with which we teach them to respond to it—all this provides admirable opportunities of wearing out a soul by attrition.

If, on the other hand, the middle years prove prosperous, our position is even stronger. Prosperity knits a man to the World. He feels that he is "finding his place in it," while really it is finding its place in him. His increasing reputation, widening circle of acquaintances, his sense of importance, the growing pressure of absorbing and agreeable work, build up in him a sense of being really at home in earth, which is just what we want. That is why we must often wish long life to our patients; seventy years is not a day too much for the difficult task of unraveling their souls from Heaven and building up a firm attachment to the earth.

So inveterate is their appetite for Heaven that our best method, at this stage, of attaching them to earth is to make them believe that earth can be turned into Heaven at some future date by politics or eugenics or "science" or psychology, or what not. Real worldliness is a work of time—assisted, of course, by pride, for we teach them to describe the creeping death as good sense or Maturity or Experience. It is obvious that to the Enemy human birth is important chiefly as the qualification for human death, and death solely as the gate to that other kind of life. Whatever you do, keep your patient as safe as you possibly can.

Your affectionate uncle,
Screwtape

Short this World and go long the Hereafter.

The Present

> *Do not worry about tomorrow, for tomorrow will worry about itself. Each day has enough trouble of its own.*
> — Prophet Jesus (PBUH)

The Prophet was walking past a garden. He turned to his friends and said, "Do you see these flowers which have blossomed? They don't know whether the sun will rise tomorrow or not. They don't know whether they will get water or not, but today they have blossomed in their joy."

It is an old story, this ceaseless struggle with time. We either longingly wish for it to return or anxiously wait for it to arrive. But the truth is that no one will bring back the years, and we are arrogant to think that time will meet us at our convenience sometime in the future. No one knows about tomorrow.

In the commotion of life, we tend to forget about our own mortality and the sometimes suddenness of death. We just assume life will continue to follow the path it began to take. So as we become preoccupied with temporal thoughts, time slips away like sand through an hourglass.

This has been a year where several unexpected tragedies have reminded me to not let time glide on quietly. Life is only available in the present.

There's a lot to look forward to in 2017, but I will take each day as it comes. For, as per C. S. Lewis, the present is all lit up with eternal rays—the point at which time touches eternity.

Blossom.

"What day is it?" asked Pooh.
"It's today," squeaked Piglet.
"My favorite day," said Pooh.

—A.A. Milne

2017

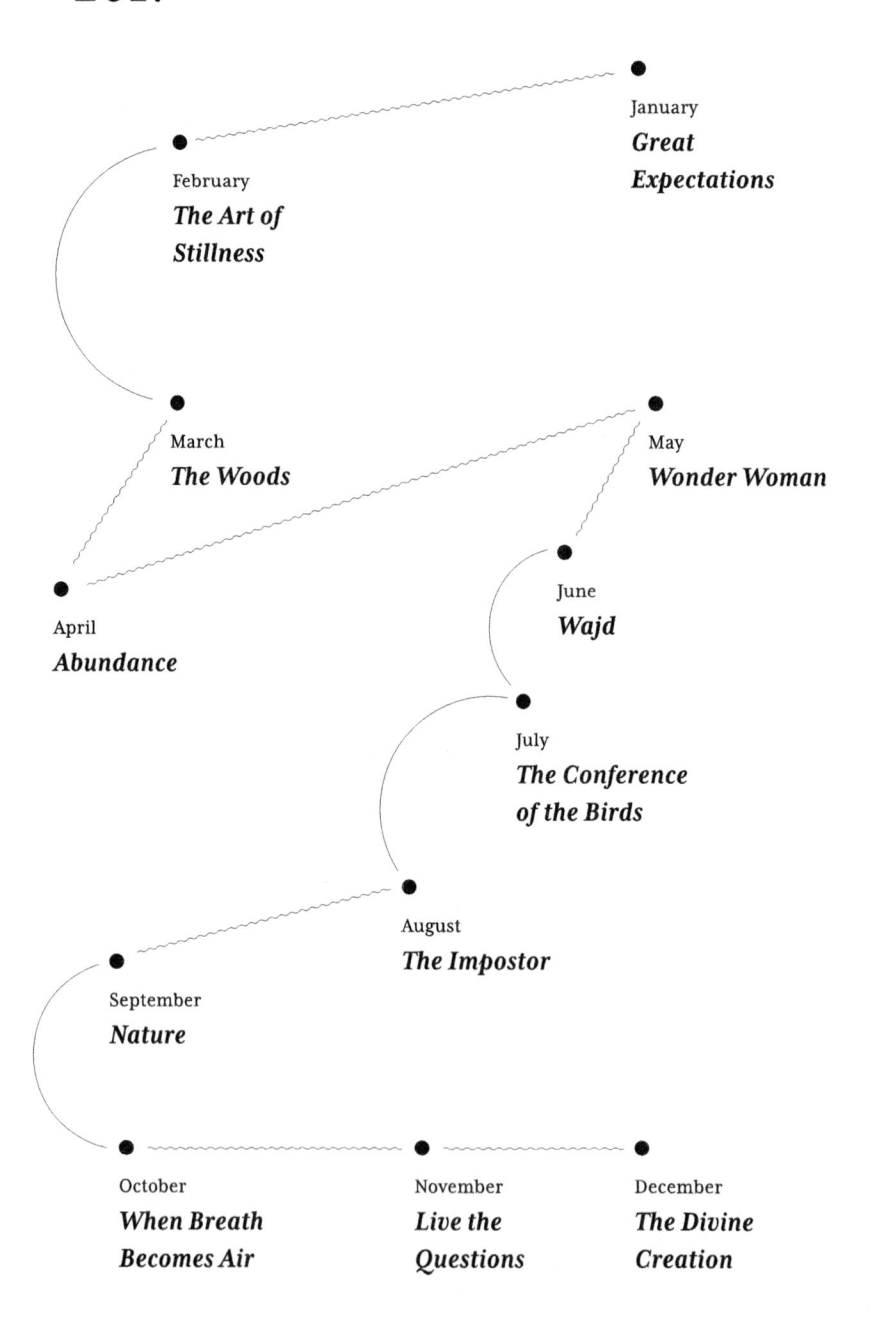

January
Great Expectations

February
The Art of Stillness

March
The Woods

April
Abundance

May
Wonder Woman

June
Wajd

July
The Conference of the Birds

August
The Impostor

September
Nature

October
When Breath Becomes Air

November
Live the Questions

December
The Divine Creation

Great Expectations

When I first read Charles Dickens' *Great Expectations*, I didn't fully fathom the genius of it. I was in high school and saw it as a traditional unrequited love story. Not until I experienced many of the common concerns of growing up—falling in love, seeking acceptance, and longing for success—did I begin to grasp the essence of the novel—an epic coming of age story. All of these themes are intricately woven into the narrative.

Great Expectations depicts the personal growth and development of Pip. From his youth to adulthood, Dickens takes us through many changes in his personality, shaped by the events and characters that influence him. Dickens portrays a bewildered world, not unlike our own, in which wealth and success hold meaning and sway. The beautiful Estella is at the top of the societal order, and Pip desires to become a part of it to acquire her. But Estella lacks judgment and remains impervious to him. When Pip realizes that his life's purpose was merely an illusion, an internal struggle forces him to redefine his values.

The novel ends not fulfilling any great expectations, but with Pip rising to a new self-awareness. By losing everything that blind ambition caused him to desire, he wins happiness and freedom. A moral regeneration leads him to understand the true worth of people and things. Thus, life takes on a new meaning.

I used to equate "success" with wealth accumulation and social status. If I could also save the world or champion a noble cause along the way, then that would be super. I was keen on establishing my place in the world. My work was my center. The quest to reach to the top defined me. Anything that advanced my goal made me happy, and anything that hindered me made me sad. The gap between my life's ambition and reality was filled with great expectations.

I hustled along. There were things to do, places to go, people to meet. Striving for the future helped me to escape the weariness of the present. Because there was so much I wanted to accomplish, I always felt confined by time. But subconsciously, I enjoyed telling people about my busyness.

According to writer Alain de Botton, one of the most interesting things about success is that we think we know what it means. Yet our ideas about what it means to live successfully are often not our own. Modern society places immense pressure on defining success in material or worldly terms—wealth, fame, position, or power. This affects what we want and how we view ourselves and others. We grade people based on their achievements. "He is successful" is understood to mean that "he is rich." But it shouldn't be this way.

In *The City of God*, St. Augustine wrote, "It's a sin to judge any man by his post." It's the person, not the job, that should count. Studies have shown there is no clear positive correlation between wealth and happiness. If we can meet our basic financial needs, money adds little to our level of fulfillment. This explains why our pursuit of material goals proves less satisfying when we finally attain them. And there's the crux. Today's definition of success needs serious realignment.

My unknowing twenty-year-old self sought to live an ideal I had sucked in from other people. My notion of success was based on superficial impressions, rather than my own sense of purpose. Like Pip, I misconstrued everything, including my heart's desire.

Thankfully, my reorientation did not spring from a midlife crisis or an emotional breakdown. As I developed a deeper understanding of the world and our existence, my perspective changed. At twenty-eight, unmarried, with no kids, no debt, and enough savings to support me for a few years, I quit my job as a prop trader. I aimed to create a life that reflected my values and would satisfy my soul.

In short, I traded money for meaning.

"How we spend our days, is, of course, how we spend our lives," observed writer Annie Dillard. To me, a life of presence is more precious than a life of promise. I decided how I want to live and went about finding a way to make a living within that way of life.

I'm very nuanced about what the word "success" means to me now. I still do what I love and work very hard, but life doesn't feel like work anymore. I no longer mistake "doing" for "being" and feel closer to my natural rhythm. My faith is now my center of strength. And it has been well said that all is well with the faithful, whatever the circumstance.

The whole future lies in uncertainty. So I stopped trying to control, even predict, where I'm going. I surrendered the reins to my life once I realized that I was never in control in the first place. I'm happy to let the universe move about. I'm now living in a comfortable space that exists between the past and the future, and I quite like it. Here, it's all about the journey, and I trust the path I'm on. As the poet Anatole France wrote, "If the path be beautiful, let us not ask where it leads." The last four years have been the most fulfilling and rewarding, both personally and professionally.

The lesson here: we must not confuse the impulse toward self-improvement with cravings for material success. To improve our circumstances, we should strive to improve our character.

The Art of Stillness

Why do people feel so rushed? Everybody, everywhere seems to be so busy. In Thorsten Veblen's day, an American economist and witty critic of capitalism during the late nineteenth-century, leisure was a "badge of honor" for the moneyed class. Today, to be pressed for time has become a sign of prosperity and an indicator of social status. Most people are inclined to claim busyness as their "badge of honor."

Part of the reason for this is that we consider time in relation to money. Hours are financially quantified, which creates an urgency to make every moment count. Psychologists find that when people are paid more to work, they tend to work longer hours, because working becomes a more profitable use of their time. When economies grow and incomes rise, people worry more about spending their time wisely. This "time-is-money" mindset explains why the tempo of life in rich countries is faster than that of poor countries, leaving us exasperated. A winner-takes-all society, one that emphasizes achievement over affiliation, tells us the point of life is to get *somewhere*, creating stressful feelings of time scarcity. The World Health Organization has warned that "stress will be the health epidemic of the twenty-first century."

In *The Art of Stillness: Adventures in Going Nowhere*, celebrated travel writer Pico Iyer makes a strong case for the urgent need to slow down and go nowhere but inside ourselves. He writes the following:

> We've lost our Sundays, our weekends, our nights off—our holy days, as some would have it; our bosses, junk mailers, our parents can find us wherever we are, at any time of day or night.

> More and more of us feel like emergency-room physicians, permanently on call, required to heal ourselves but unable to find the prescription for all the clutter on our desk... In an age of speed, nothing could be more invigorating than going slow. In an age of distraction, nothing can feel more luxurious than paying attention. And in an age of constant movement, nothing is more urgent than sitting still.

The great saints, the poets of East Asia, the philosophers of ancient Greece and Rome all made stillness the center of their lives. But the need for being in one place as a way of cutting through the noise and finding fresh time and energy has never been as vital as it is right now. We have more and more information and less and less time and space to make sense of it. There's no questioning the need for clarity and focus. As Iyer states:

> Not many years ago, it was access to information and movement that seemed our greatest luxury. Nowadays it's often freedom from information, the chance to sit still that feels like the ultimate prize. The more facts come streaming in on us, the less time we have to process any one of them. The ability to gather information, which used to be so crucial, is now far less important than the ability to sift through it. It's easy to feel as if we're standing two inches away from a huge canvas that's noisy and crowded and changing with every microsecond. It's only by stepping farther back and standing still that we can begin

to see what that canvas (which is our life) really means, and to take in the larger picture.

According to Iyer, stillness is not just an indulgence for those with enough resources—it's a necessity for anyone who wishes to gather less visible resources. It's only by taking our self away from clutter and distraction that we can reclaim our senses and begin to make sense of the world and everything in it. And it's only by sitting still that we are able to draw upon what we've collected in our deeper moments.

> *It is easy in the world to*
> *live after the world's opinion;*
> *it is easy in solitude to*
> *live after our own;*
> *but the great man is he who*
> *in the midst of the crowd*
> *keeps with perfect sweetness*
> *the independence of solitude*
>
> — Ralph Waldo Emerson

The Woods

Our life is frittered away by detail. Simplify, simplify.
— Henry David Thoreau

In the summer of 1845, a twenty-eight-year-old Henry David Thoreau went to Walden Pond, a sixty-two-acre body of water in Concord, Massachusetts, to live in a place belonging to his close friend, Ralph Waldo Emerson. Part experiment, part spiritual quest, Thoreau wanted to immerse himself in nature in the hope to gain a more objective understanding of how people live or ought to live. Thoreau states:

> I went to the woods because I wished to live deliberately, to front only the essential facts of life, and see if I could not learn what it had to teach, and not, when I came to die, discover that I had not lived. I did not wish to live what was not life, living is so dear; nor did I wish to practice resignation, unless it was quite necessary. I wanted to live deep and suck out all the marrow of life, to live so sturdily and Spartan-like as to put to rout all that was not life, to cut a broad swath and shave close, to drive life into a corner, and reduce it to its lowest terms, and, if it proved to be mean, why then to get the whole and genuine meanness of it, and publish its meanness to the world; or if it were sublime, to know it by experience, and be able to give a true account of it in my next excursion.

Walden, unquestionably Thoreau's most significant work, takes the reader through the seasons at the pond and the experience of living life more simply. Thoreau was skeptical that any outward improvement of life can bring inner peace and contentment. He paid attention to what he owned and what owned him, as well as to how he spent his time. He believed it is desirable to live so compactly and preparedly that, "if an enemy takes the town, he can walk out the gate empty-handed without anxiety... My greatest skill has been to want but little."

In a world where most people measure their worth in terms of what they own, Thoreau discovered the ownership of material possessions beyond the basic necessities of life to be an obstacle rather than an advantage. "Most of the luxuries, and many of the so-called comforts of life, are not only not indispensable, but hindrances to the elevation of mankind," he wrote.

Through careful observation, Thoreau emphasizes the importance of solitude, contemplation, and closeness to nature as a remedy for the mass of people who have become disenchanted with their everyday lives. His aim is to have them consider their own possibilities for improving their situations, for overcoming their lives of "quiet desperation," as shown in the following quote:

> I learned this, at least, by my experiment; that if one advances confidently in the direction of his dreams, and endeavors to live the life which he has imagined, he will meet with a success unexpected in common hours. He will put some things behind, will pass an invisible boundary; new, universal, and more liberal laws will begin to establish themselves around and within him,

and he will live with the license of a higher order of beings. As he simplifies his life, the laws of the universe will appear less complex; solitude will not be solitude, poverty will not be poverty, nor weakness weakness. If you have built castles in the air, your work need not be lost; that is where they should be. Now put the foundations under them.

Love the earth and sun and animals. Despise riches, give alms to everyone that asks. Stand up for the stupid and crazy. Devote your income and labor to others. And your flesh shall be a great poem.

— Walt Whitman

Abundance

> *Even after all this time,*
> *The sun never says to the earth,*
> *"You owe me."*
> *Look what happens with a love like that,*
> *It lights the whole sky.*
> — Hafiz

At the peak of every commodity supercycle in history, humans have thought our insatiable demand for resources will exhaust the earth's crust of just about every metal and mineral. In 1798, Thomas Malthus warned of the dangers of population growth, arguing that the power of demographics will be superior to the power of the earth's ability to provide sustenance.

But even as our numbers swelled from one billion in 1800 to over seven billion today, a surprising thing happened: nature did not go bankrupt. Mother earth, it seems, has much to give. There have still been famines. But in all such instances, the loss of life was a result of failure in human action—botched policies, hoarding or corruption, and a lack of cross-border aid. The world, as a whole, has never been short of food. Inadequate production is not to blame for the 800 million people who go to bed hungry each night. According to the United Nations World Food Programme, one-third of all food produced globally (1.3 billion tons) is never consumed. The food simply goes to waste. How is it that we are like this?

From the earth's abundance springs life. Yet we seem to squander our amazing inheritance. Poor nutrition causes nearly half of the deaths in children under five—that's 3.1 million children each year. One in nine people on this earth do not have enough food to lead a healthy and active life. In America of all places, 35 million people are hungry and don't know where their next meal will come from— 13 million of whom are children. As actor Jeff Bridges poignantly observed, "If another country were doing this to our children, we'd be at war."

What, then, should we make of this carelessness? Why do we withhold the bounty of life? Why can't we give like the sun, give to everyone equally and unconditionally? It is not the world's resources, but our hearts and mind that are finite. It is not the neglect of resources, but the neglect of people that is likely to end very badly.

> *See, O Humans!*
> *The birds flying high in the skies*
> *Just see what they do*
> *Neither do they hoard their food*
> *Nor do they starving die*
> *Has anyone ever seen*
> *Birds dying of hunger?*
> *It's only humans who hoard*
> *And humans who of hunger die*
> — Bulleh Shah

Wonder Woman

"Can you come home?"

"Why? You know Steve's in town."

"I'm worried."

"What happened?"

"I went to the clinic today to see Dr. Annie, and she said the delivery needs to be medically coaxed. The baby has not gained any weight in the past two weeks, and my placenta is calcifying. She is concerned the baby will start losing weight. If that happens, it will be more difficult to try for natural birth. She said she wants to induce me tomorrow."

"Tomorrow?!"

"Yes, tomorrow. Can you please come home early?"

Friday, May 26

So we left Zaynab with my parents and drove to the hospital. But it actually felt like we were about to check into a hotel for a staycation. The birthing process could take six hours or up to three days, the doctor said. "We want to give the baby as much time as she needs and let nature take its course." So my overzealous wife, Saniha, packed a whole suitcase with all of our belongings.

The feeling that we were about to have a baby had not yet overcome me. My mind was stuck on a presentation I was scheduled to deliver to one of our core clients in a few days. I just prayed that the baby would arrive before then.

Thankfully, the hospital room was pretty and spacious, so I had no trouble adapting myself to what would become my new work environment. I yanked out my laptop and started typing away as my wife was being given an intravenous line to start having mild contractions.

"Feel anything yet?"

"Nope."

Normally, doctors induce and send the mother home. But because Saniha had a Cesarean birth for our first daughter, the medical staff needed to closely monitor her to ensure the scar on her uterus from her previous C-section did not reopen during labor, which would put her and the baby at serious risk. So I made myself comfortable.

"I can feel it now. Ooohh."

Dr. Annie arrived late in the evening, and my wife was only 1 cm dilated.

"How much does she need to be?"

"10 cm."

I chuckled and sunk in my couch. "Just go to sleep," I thought. Saniha was doing fine and wanted to get some rest too.

Saturday, May 27

As I snored through the night, Saniha kept waking up from the labor pains. Her contractions were getting stronger, and she started feeling backaches— a positive sign that the baby was moving lower.

In the morning, the nurses asked if she wanted to take an epidural to block the pain, but Saniha refused. I looked at her, astonished.

"Why?"

"I won't be able to tell the difference between normal labor pains and if my scar has reopened. I'm scared. I don't want to disconnect from the feeling of giving birth to my baby."

But what she described as fear was actually strength. As the renowned pediatrician Dr. William Sears so eloquently said, "How you approach birth is intimately connected with how you approach life." Living in a superficial era that has numbed our senses, what could be more courageous than experiencing childbirth with all the agony and awareness?

"You're 3 cm dilated."

Sunday, May 28

Saniha's labor was still going slow, so slow that Dr. Annie phoned in to increase the dosage to quicken the contractions. Now, they were really stepping up. She started pacing around the room as I relaxed on the couch, pulling up charts and writing notes.

The midwife helped Saniha try new positions to ease the discomfort and also gave her a birthing ball. Her bouncing around was quite distracting, so I figured I should just take a break and be more involved. I offered words of support from time to time although I'm not sure how welcome they were.

"Do you feel a spiritual uplifting?"

All I got was a cold stare.

Hours later, I was happy to see Dr. Annie return.

"Why is it taking so long?"

"Everything comes at its appointed hour."

I was moved by her words. Saniha desperately wanted to have a natural birth, so she had spent months looking for a doctor who would be willing to support her the whole way. In that moment, it felt to me that she had made the right choice. I didn't think much of it before, but now, I understood why this was so important to her.

Before Dr. Annie left, she broke Saniha's water bag.

"Fatima should be here tomorrow."

Monday, May 29

At this point, seven babies had been born in our ward since our time there. Saniha was counting. She also became good friends with all the midwives and acquired enough knowledge that she could deliver our third child all by herself at home if she wanted to.

It was a nerve-racking few days, and although it seems incredibly selfish to mention it, I was exhausted from working out of the hospital. Saniha's contractions were more intense now and occurring almost back to back. And because she wasn't able to move about much (plugged to the baby monitor and all the intravenous lines), she was getting very uncomfortable and beginning to lose it. Despite my feeling of uselessness, I pretended to stay calm and supportive.

"Everything will be fine."

Professor Barbara Katz Rothman was correct in saying, "Birth is not only about making babies. Birth is about making mothers: strong, competent, capable mothers who trust themselves and know their inner strength."

Dr. Annie arrived at 5 p.m. "I'm not leaving till we have your baby."

Saniha smiled, took a long, deep breath and exhaled, as if replacing every molecule of air within her. I could tell she was ready.

"Shall we try? You're 10 cm dilated now."

Saniha's womb had softened from the pain of labor. And with every contraction, I could see her reach deeper inside of herself and pull energy and strength from a reservoir that I never knew existed, a place only a woman can access in and through birth.

But after hours of trying, baby Fatima remained comfortably turned on her side, and refused to find that opening to be born. Dr. Annie even tried using a vacuum, but to no avail. I prodded Saniha along with reassuring words because I knew she wanted this badly and had given it her all. I never felt prouder of her than at that moment.

It was nearly midnight, and Saniha made a quick, sensible decision.

"Dr. Annie, let's do the C-section."

Tuesday, May 30

The emergency team was called, and everyone prepped for surgery. I was handed green scrubs to wear and told to wait outside. They'd call me in just before they would start.

In those fleeting moments, I started to panic. It was strange. I felt so afraid. *What if something goes wrong?* All these negative thoughts kept pouring into my head. I knew this is stupid; it's a simple operation. But I couldn't prevent my heart from sinking in my chest with the fright of losing Saniha. Fatima didn't even cross my mind.

"Come on in."

I regained my composure, wiped my tears, and walked into the OR to find my wife ready to be cut open. I went behind the curtain and held Saniha's hand during the C-section, but it felt more like she was holding mine.

Shortly after, I watched Dr. Annie force the baby out of her mother's womb. As I peered over the curtain, I was overcome with joy and relief. I thanked God incessantly. Fatima was captivating, just like her name.

There is a special sweetness in being able to participate in the essence of creation, even if only as a bystander. When Fatima grows up, I want to tell her this story, how her mother practically gave birth to her twice—

first natural and then C-section. I want her to know it's not that birth is painful, but that women are strong, strong, so incredibly strong.

"I love you."

Wajd

> *Beware of confining yourself to a particular belief and denying all else, for much good would elude you—indeed, the knowledge of reality would elude you.*
> — Ibn Arabi

Muhyiddin Ibn Arabi, also known as the "Great Master," is one of the most influential Muslim thinkers in history. Born in Spain in 1165, he traveled from city to city in pursuit of knowledge, eventually settling in Damascus, where he taught and wrote. He dedicated his life to the spiritual path and left behind several hundred books and treatises on theology, philosophy, psychology, cosmology, and mysticism.

In *Imaginal Worlds*, a great summary of Ibn Arabi's extraordinary corpus of work, author William Chittick writes:

> It is difficult to explain in a few words what is special about Ibn Arabi's teachings. He stands as a grand monument to the possibilities of preserving rationality while simultaneously transcending it, and he could not but act as a beacon for those looking for an exit from the impasses of modern thought.

Ibn Arabi believed rational analysis was not sufficient to attain complete knowledge of the world. He called for a harmony between the labyrinth of reason and spiritual perception. God is not a hypothesis that can simply be dispensed with. Ibn Arabi perceived a wide gulf between the formal knowledge of rational thinkers and the folk of *wajd*, those with illuminated wisdom.

In Ibn Arabi's terminology, *wujud* refers to the whole cosmos, to everything that exists, and *wajd* is an "unveiling," or the opening of the door to Divine knowledge. Anyone who experiences *wajd* attains a new sense of awareness and some luminous knowledge from the object of his finding, *wujud*. The spiritual station is realized only through a relentless struggle to subdue the ego and through the complete passing away of the self and its attributes.

Possibly the most distinctive characteristic of Ibn Arabi's teachings is the importance he places on imagination. Only by escaping the bounds of the intellect and placing imagination near the center of our consciousness will we be able to grasp the indefinable and unknowable grounds of everything that exists. "He who does not know the status of imagination has no knowledge whatsoever," the Great Master decreed.

So in human development our aim should be *wajd*—to seek Divine inspiration and reach the degree of intellectual vision that breaks the manacles of conventional thinking and gives us true insight into the Reality of things.

"O God, show us things as they are."

The Conference of the Birds

The birds of the world gather together for a conference to discuss all the trials and tribulations of their existence. The hoopoe, the wisest of them all, says to his avian brethren:

> Birds!
> Look at the troubles happening in our world
> Anarchy, discontent, upheaval!
> Desperate fights over territory, water, and food!
> Poisoned air! Unhappiness!
> I fear we are lost. We must do something!
> I've seen the world. I know many secrets.
> Listen to me: I know of a king who has all the answers.
> We must go and find him.

But the birds are deterred by the prospect of a long and arduous quest. Each presents an elaborate excuse. The hawk says he is content serving the royal court and hunting for their sport; the nightingale says she is so drowned in love of flowers that she can't live without them; the owl says he is too wise to believe in fantasies; the duck only desires the sanctuary of her cozy pond; the heron prefers to live by the desolate shoreline; the finch fears he is too frail, and so on.

The hoopoe dispels their objections with allegorical stories and great wisdom and exhorts them to join her on the journey to Mount Qaf in search for their one true king, Simorgh. Their quest takes them through seven valleys, each of which prepares them for their own becoming.

In the first valley of the quest, they learn, through much striving and grieving, to cast aside their beliefs and purify the heart for its sacred encounter. In the valley of love, they realize that love, actually, has nothing to do with reason. The valley of understanding teaches the birds that worldly knowledge is temporary, but wisdom endures. In the valley of detachment, the birds are roused to let go of everything they cling to so that they can feel safe and better about themselves. They shed their desire to be in "control" as they come to terms with life's realities, accepting whatever comes their way with grace and humility. Then, stripped of the illusion that we, alone, are the center of our little universe, the birds realize in the valley of unity that we are all bound together—that there is, in fact, unity in diversity. Entering the sixth valley of bewilderment, the birds feel that they know nothing. To cross the final valley of death, every form of the ego must be sacrificed, even the conceit of rectitude. The birds come to realize their nothingness. Out of thousands of birds, only thirty reach Mount Qaf by the end. Many give up along the Way; others perish.

The king's palace is glorious, but it is empty, except for the mirrors on all the walls. Around and around they fly, but Simorgh is nowhere to be seen. Then, suddenly, a strange feeling of joy overcomes the surviving birds. They realize the significance of the mirrors. They have found the Simorgh after all: it is looking back at them in their own reflections. They realize that what they were seeking, the ideal leader who could guide them and solve the world's problems, was within them all along—that Simorgh is, in fact, each of them and all of them.

The poem, *The Conference of the Birds*, by Farid ud-Din Attar (1145–1221) is a text of living wisdom. Writers from Rumi to Dante to Borges have been drawn to it as an allegory for the journey to discover one's true self. Of Attar, Rumi wrote, "He traveled all seven cities of love. While I'm still at the bend of its first valley."

Attar was a pharmacist in Nishapur, Iran. The legend is that a dervish came to his shop one day asking for alms. But Attar was too occupied to serve him. After waiting for quite some time, the dervish rebuked him, "If you are so busy in life, how will you make time for death?"

Agitated, Attar replied, "I will die the same as you." That moment, the dervish threw himself on the ground, invoked the Divine, and his soul left his body. This act of power and devotion made such an impression on Attar that he left his shop and began traveling in search of wisdom.

Attar's death, as with his life, is subject to mystery. It is said he was taken prisoner by the Mongols during the invasion of Nishapur. Someone came along one day and offered a thousand pieces of silver to free him. Attar told his captors not to sell him for that price. The Mongols refused the ransom, thinking to gain an even greater sum of money.

Later, another person came, this time offering only a sack of straw. "Sell me to him," said Attar. "For that is all I am worth." Outraged, the Mongols struck him with a sword and gave Attar endless life.

> The home we seek is in eternity;
> The Truth we seek is like a shoreless sea,
> Of which your paradise is but a drop.
> This ocean can be yours; why should you stop
> Beguiled by dreams of evanescent dew?
> The secrets of the sun are yours, but you
> Content yourself with motes trapped in its beams.
> Turn to what truly lives, reject what seems—
> Which matters more, the body or the soul?
> Be whole: desire and journey to the Whole.

The Impostor

Some years ago, Neil Gaiman, a prolific and award-winning author known for an array of works, was invited to a gathering of great people: artists, scientists, writers, and discoverers of things. And he felt that at any moment, they would realize that he didn't qualify to be among these people, all of whom had really astonishing achievements.

On his second night there, feeling out of place, Gaiman moved to the back of the hall and started talking to a very nice, polite, old man while a musical performance was going on. They spoke about several things, including their shared first name. The elderly gentleman pointed to the crowd of people and said, "I just look at all these people, and I think, what the heck am I doing here? They've made amazing things. I just went where I was sent."

And Gaiman replied, "Yes. But you were the first man on the moon. I think that counts for something." And he felt a bit better because if Neil Armstrong felt like an impostor, maybe everyone did. "Maybe there weren't any grown-ups," he thought to himself. "Only people who had worked hard and also got lucky and were slightly out of their depth, all of us doing the best job we could, which is all we can really hope for."

According to philosopher Alain de Botton, the root cause of impostor syndrome is a hugely unhelpful picture of what other people are really like. Here's an excerpt from his collection of work, *The Book of Life*:

> We feel like impostors not because we are uniquely flawed, but because we fail to imagine how deeply flawed everyone else must necessarily also be

beneath a more or less polished surface. We know ourselves from the inside, but others only from the outside. We're constantly aware of all our anxieties, doubts and idiocies from within. Yet all we know of others is what they happen to do and tell us, a far narrower, and more edited source of information... It means that whenever we encounter a stranger we're not really encountering a stranger, we're in fact encountering someone who is—in spite of the surface evidence to the contrary—in basic ways very much like us—and that therefore nothing fundamental stands between us and the possibility of responsibility, success, and fulfilment.

I have been an impostor my whole life.

As a kid who wanted to be a doctor, I pretended to be Doogie Howser. When that plan failed and I decided to be a lawyer, I acted like Muhammad Ali Jinnah and imagined myself being Pakistan's next prime minister. Once I began my career as a bank teller, I put on a dashing suit and told my friends that I was a banker. Soon after, when I realized that I actually wanted to be an investor, I started posing as a hedge fund manager. I read everything worth reading and knew every price worth tracking. I pretended my monthly salary was a "subscription" into my "fund" that I started trading.

I did not have the experience or network to set up a hedge fund, so I launched Stray Reflections instead, which made it possible for me to engage in deliberate practice to become a great macro investor. I wanted to use the freedom to think, write, and trade as if I was running my own hedge fund. Now, I thrive on the competition, the intellectual challenge of forecasting macro trends, enduring in this environment by putting up consistently high returns.

Given my unorthodox background, I didn't think I was anything like the people I admired. But the inherent danger of believing you're not good enough is that it will become self-fulfilling. So I thought I'd just fake it till I made it. As the American playwright Tennessee Williams said, "What's talent but the ability to get away with something?" The downside is that I still sometimes feel like a fraud, living in the fear that someday, people will realize that I'm not as smart or competent as they think I am. But it is reassuring to know I'm not alone.

Poet Maya Angelou wrote eleven books, but each time, she thought, "Uh oh, they're going to find out now. I've run a game on everybody, and they're going to find me out." Straight after winning best actor for The Accused in 1999, Jodie Foster was worried she'd have to give her Oscar back. And after attending a Harvard University speech called "Feeling Like a Fraud," Sheryl Sandberg said, "I felt like that my whole life."

I've come to believe the only way to overcome the impostor syndrome is to work hard and deliver the goods. I want to show clients how macro thinking and money management can be gracefully and profitably intertwined. Then, maybe I'll convince myself too.

Nature

> *The exceeding beauty of the earth, in her splendor of life, yields a new thought with every petal. The hours when the mind is absorbed by beauty are the only hours when we really live. This is real life, and all else is illusion, or mere endurance. To be beautiful and to be calm, without mental fear, is the ideal of nature.*
> — Richard Jefferies

An investor is a professional observer. In one sense, it has never been easier: we have never had this many tools and information at our fingertips, not to mention the ability to keep an eye on what's going on globally. But in another sense, it has never been more difficult: our brain is easily fatigued when trying to ascertain subtle signals from noisy news flows. Trapped behind our Bloomberg screen, we have become isolated from everything, including our own increasingly abstract thoughts.

"In order to understand the world, one has to turn away from it on occasion," French-Algerian philosopher Albert Camus wrote in the 1940s as he contemplated the modern megalopolis. But where should we flee from the traffic and high-rises to clear our mental windshield?

For all of recorded history, people have been writing about their profound experiences in nature. Science is now proving what we all know as an elemental truth of existence: when we get closer to nature—be it untouched wilderness or a backyard tree—we do our body and overstressed brains a favor. Not only do we feel refreshed, but our cognitive functioning improves too.

Research by psychologist David Strayer of the University of Utah finds that being in nature allows the prefrontal cortex, the brain's command center, to rest and recover. When the prefrontal cortex quiets down, the brain's default network kicks in, which permits a more reflective state, enhances higher-order thinking, restores mental energy, and boosts creativity. And it doesn't take much to achieve that: short doses of nature, such as walking in a city park or any green space for as little as 25 minutes, is enough to give our prefrontal cortex a break.

Emerson insisted long ago that "nature is medicinal." People living near natural surroundings or more green space have fewer stress hormones circulating in the blood and a lower incidence of health problems, including depression, migraines, anxiety, heart disease, diabetes, and asthma.

The natural world can offer us more than beauty, yet we have disconnected ourselves from it in our technology-filled urban world. Before nature vanishes bit by bit, let us not forget the sage words of Thoreau: "All nature is doing her best each moment to make us well—she exists for no other end. Do not resist her."

When Breath Becomes Air

> *You that seek what life is in death,*
> *Now find it air that once was breath.*
> *New names unknown, old names gone;*
> *Till time end bodies, but souls none.*
> *Reader! Then make time, while you be,*
> *But steps to your eternity.*
> — Baron Brooke Fulke Greville

My head leaned back on my mother's shoulder; my eyes gazed outside at my three-year-old daughter, Zaynab, speaking in the air as she played in the garden. Someone was being scolded, I could tell, from the way she held her hands on her waist. I have faced her wrath.

"How much of this will I remember?" I asked.

"How much of what?" my mom replied, pouring us tea.

"This. Zaynab. Our time together. We pour so much love and energy into our kids, and they bring us so much happiness. How much will I remember of these moments when I'm older? How much do you remember of us?"

I could tell that the answer was not much. She summed up my entire childhood in six minutes. The few stories lacked any detail. There was only a sense of what Jawad was like. Her day-to-day striving, outpouring, and receiving... all forgotten. It made her slightly uncomfortable, I felt. That was not my intention.

"What does it mean?" I wondered. "What's the point?"

The next morning, I picked up a book from my shelf that I had been meaning to read for a while—*When Breath Becomes Air*, an intimate memoir of a young doctor with great ambition who comes face-to-face with his own mortality. In a letter to a friend, the author writes, "That's what I'm aiming for, I think. Not the sensationalism of dying, and not exhortations to gather rosebuds, but: Here's what lies up ahead on the road." I felt drawn to its premise.

Passionate about science and writing, Paul Kalanithi majored in English and biology at Stanford and went on to pursue a master's degree in philosophy from Cambridge before graduating from the Yale School of Medicine. He was interested in discovering where "biology, morality, literature and philosophy intersect," so he chose neurosurgery, the most difficult specialism of all, drawn by its "unforgiving call to perfection." He states the following:

> I had started in this career, in part, to pursue death: to grasp it, uncloak it, and see eye-to-eye, unblinking. Neurosurgery attracted me as much for its intertwining of brain and consciousness as for its intertwining of life and death. I had thought that a life spent in the space between the two would grant me not merely a stage for compassionate action but an elevation of my own being: getting as far away from petty materialism, from self-important trivia, getting right there, to the heart of the matter, to truly life and death decisions and struggles... surely a kind of transcendence would be found there? I was

driven less by achievement than by trying to
understand, in earnest: What makes human
life meaningful?

And then, at age thirty-six, at the peak of a career bursting with
potential, the unthinkable happens. Paul finds himself a patient at
the very hospital where he worked as a neurosurgeon, diagnosed
with stage IV lung cancer. He doesn't know it yet, but he has twenty-
two months left. Torn between being a doctor and being a patient,
delving into medical science and turning back to literature for answers,
he struggles, while facing his own death, to rebuild his old life—or perhaps
find a new one. His whole sense of identity is shaken. "My carefully
planned and hard-won future no longer existed." He goes on to say:

> As a doctor, I had had some sense of what patients
> with life-changing illnesses faced—and it was
> exactly these moments I had wanted to explore
> with them. Shouldn't terminal illness, then, be
> the perfect gift to that young man who had
> wanted to understand death? What better way
> to understand it than to live it? But I'd had no
> idea how hard it would be, how much terrain I
> would have to explore, map, settle. I'd always
> imagined the doctor's work as something like
> connecting two pieces of railroad track, allowing
> a smooth journey for the patient. I hadn't expected
> the prospect of facing my own mortality to be so
> disorienting, so dislocating... looking into my
> own soul, I found the tools too brittle, the fire
> too weak, to forge even my own conscience.

Lost in a featureless wasteland of his own mortality and finding no traction in the realm of scientific studies, it's literature that brings Paul back to life during this time:

> The monolithic uncertainty of my future was deadening; everywhere I turned, the shadow of death obscured the meaning of any action. I remember the moment when my overwhelming unease yielded, when that seemingly impassable sea of uncertainty parted. I woke up in pain, facing another day—no project beyond breakfast seemed tenable. *I can't go on*, I thought, and immediately, its antiphon responded, completing Samuel Beckett's seven words, words I had learned long ago as an undergraduate: *I'll go on*. I got out of bed and took a step forward, repeating the phrase over and over: "I can't go on. I'll go on." That morning, I made a decision: I would push myself to return to the OR. Why? Because I could. Because that's who I was. Because I would have to learn to live in a different way, seeing death as an imposing itinerant visitor but knowing that even if I'm dying, until I actually die, I am still living.

After much deliberation, Paul and his wife, Lucy, decide to have a child. "Don't you think saying goodbye to your child will make your death more painful?" she asks. He responds, simply, "Wouldn't it be great if it did?"

As he nears the end, Paul comes to believe that life is about striving, not about avoiding suffering. And that life's meaning, its virtue, has something to do with the depth of the relationships we form. "Human knowledge is never contained in one person," Paul writes. "It grows from the relationships we create between each other and the world, and still it is never complete. And Truth comes somewhere above all of them." That's what makes life worth living, even in the face of death and decay:

> Everyone succumbs to finitude. I suspect I am not the only one who reaches this pluperfect state. Most ambitions are either achieved or abandoned; either way, they belong to the past. The future, instead of the ladder toward the goals of life, flattens out into a perpetual present. Money, status, all the vanities the preacher of Ecclesiastes described, hold so little interest: a chasing after wind, indeed. We are never so wise as when we live in this moment.

Paul died on March 9, 2015, aged thirty-seven, with these final words for his nine-month-old daughter, Cady:

> When you come to one of the many moments in life when you must give an account of yourself, provide a ledger of what you have been, and done, and meant to the world, do not, I pray, discount that you filled a dying man's days with a sated joy, a joy unknown to me in all my prior years, a joy that does not hunger for more and more, but rests, satisfied. In this time, right now, that is an enormous thing.

As I put the book down, I was filled with an awareness blunted through the daily distraction of living: death comes for all of us. Yet we never suspect our own fragility. And so it is with my darling Zaynab, all I have with her is the present moment. That is an enormous thing.

> **I have realized that the past and future are real illusions, that they exist in the present, which is what there is and all there is.**
>
> — Alan Watts

Live the Questions

We all start out as super curious beings. It is estimated that between the ages of two and five, children ask about 40,000 questions, which help spur and accelerate learning. But then, as we grow older, we gradually ask fewer and fewer. Perhaps, our parents lose patience with us, our teachers demand answers not questions, and our bosses just want us to be silent and do our work. Before we know it, the habit of asking questions is completely wrung out of us, and we actually become afraid of questions. We keep burying them deep inside our heart.

Tony Robbins has said that the quality of your life is determined by the quality of the questions you ask. But what if questions make us ache? In the daily humdrum of life, we don't have the time to stop and probe questions that give dimension and hope and meaning to our lives. What's most perplexing is this overwhelming feeling of uneasiness in the quiet presence of our own thoughts. To renew the search for a deeper form of knowing, we have an ever-increasing need for someone to remind us of the important questions that call us.

In a fascinating TED talk on "The Psychology of Your Future Self," Harvard psychologist Dan Gilbert posed such a question:

> Human beings are works in progress that mistakenly think they're finished. The person you are right now is as transient, as fleeting and as temporary as all the people you've ever been. The one constant in our lives is change. If the person you will be in 30 years—the person for whom you

> plan your life now by working toward career goals and putting money aside in retirements plans—is invariably different from the person you are today, what makes that future person "you?" We set goals for the people we are when we set them rather than the people we become when we reach them.

According to Gilbert, this is not only wrong but also a source of much of our unhappiness. We tend to act like we know all the answers. That who we are at the present moment is the final destination of our becoming. But this particular time is only a point along our personal journey. So we must learn to be comfortable with questions—to let them guide us and help move us forward. Answers often freeze us in place.

In a 1903 letter to his protégé, the nineteen-year-old cadet and budding poet Franz Xaver Kappus, Rainer Maria Rilke wrote:

> I beg you, to have patience with everything unresolved in your heart. Try to love the questions themselves as if they were locked rooms or books written in a foreign language. Don't search for the answers, which could not be given to you now, because you would not be able to live them. And the point is to live everything. Live the questions now. Perhaps then, someday far in the future, you will gradually, without even noticing it, live your way into the answer.

This. This is how you find your way.

Wherever a man may happen to turn, whatever a man may undertake, he will always end up by returning to that path which nature has marked out for him.

— Goethe

The Divine Creation

"Read this."

I put down my cup of tea and took the phone from Hussain's hand. I thumbed up and down the screen to find a long scroll.

"What is it?"

"Just read."

Hussain is the person I feel closest to in the world. It is hard to overstate the impact he has had on my life. We live in different cities and only speak about once a month, but there is no one I trust more to give me the right advice. If I'm somewhat more spiritually inclined today than I was before, it is because of him.

Five years ago, I remember sitting in his office in an old antiquated building in Lahore. I was struggling to find my way.

"You're a writer," he told me.

"No, I'm not!" I snapped. It was my hedge fund persona that felt under attack. It was also because I knew Hussain had a gift for writing, and there's no way I could be as good as him.

Even today, I feel like I just copy and paste ideas rather than share anything that is truly original. My battle with resistance is real. But I'm not willing to give up the fight.

"Is there more tea?"

As I read the first sentence off the phone, I realized this was Hussain's writing and got excited. It had been a long time since I read anything from him. He tells the story of the Divine creation in poetic form:

> Meeting the saint, I asked my question, and he gave me a serious look; I must say that I was rendered thoughtless for a moment as though there was an earthquake and the ground beneath my feet had shook.
>
> He then looked at me and said:
>
> There was a time when the heart, soul, and spirit lived independently from one another... it was a time of separation and freedom, and there was none to stifle or smother. They were all God's favorites, each enjoying its own rank. They knew they were the favorites, so they became boastful, proud and frank.
>
> The spirit was close to God, but the soul was closer still, and although the heart was in a state of union, there existed a longing, a feeling of incompleteness in them all, that only God could fill. One day an argument broke as to who is God's favorite. The parties became violent as the argument got heated. God was approached and requested to mediate to which He agreed and

said that He would reveal the truth unto all of them naturally, so no one feels cheated.

He then said He would create man and thus ordered the angels to bring clay from the earth. He said everyone has transgressed to a point where they all need to know their place before me and their worth. So, the angels took the heart and bound it to the soul then they took the soul and sunk it into the spirit's chest. Then the angels put the heart, soul and spirit into man and God then raised man to a supreme rank, stating that this creation was his best. He then ordered the angels to put man on earth, as it is humble and has the power to reveal things worth.

Since the heart knows only union, it is the union that it seeks, and since the soil and spirit only know closeness and proximity, it is the only language they speak. And since man is from earth it is this world that he desires, its bones and flesh with the help of the mind have to fuel its earthly fires.

So you see, my son, everything revealed to itself, what it knew best. Do not for a second think that what you think or feel is trivial or is thought and felt in jest. The body and mind are natives of this world and they will always sing its praise, but the heart, soul and spirit are alien to this place and do not understand its customs, norms, and ways. The heart, soul, and spirit were favorites of God and thus have been spoiled with His love and attention, while the body and mind are unfamiliar with these emotions; to them these feelings are a strange dimension.

If you have it in you to seek God then listen to your heart, but if you want to seek the world instead, then it is the mind where you start.

You would attain to the Divine perfection. And yet, not turn your back upon the world.

— Henry Wadsworth Longfellow

2018

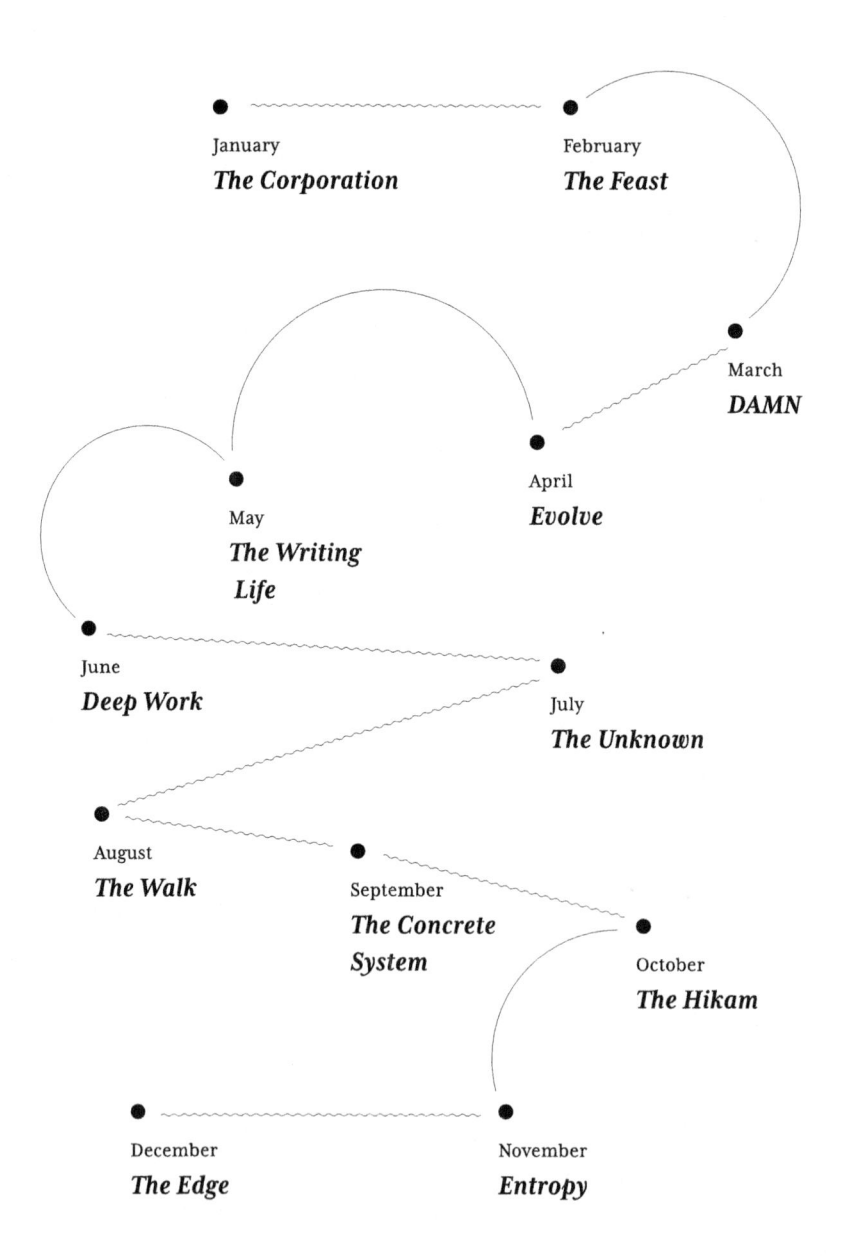

January
The Corporation

February
The Feast

March
DAMN

April
Evolve

May
The Writing Life

June
Deep Work

July
The Unknown

August
The Walk

September
The Concrete System

October
The Hikam

November
Entropy

December
The Edge

The Corporation

Like the church and monarchy in other times and places, the corporation is today's dominant institution. It is all-pervasive. But it didn't always used to be this way. In the early days of the American republic, legislators granted few corporate charters and did so only after debate. The privilege of incorporation was granted selectively and predominantly to enable activities that benefited the public, such as the construction of roads or canals—infrastructure projects that the states did not have the money to build themselves. And the states imposed conditions: limiting charters to a set number of years, setting limits on commercial interest, not allowing them to own stock in other corporations, or not allowing them to make any political contributions to influence law making. The power of large shareholders was also limited by scaled voting so that large and small investors had equal voting rights. Owners were held personally responsible for violating laws.

According to legal historian Brian Murphy, America's founding fathers saw corporations as corrupting influences on both the economy and on government. The American Revolution against the colonial British Empire was invoked because of the tyranny of the East India Company, which led to the Tea Party revolt. They viewed the company as a "state within a state" and did not want to replicate that outcome. The founding fathers were much more comfortable with city or school charters than with creating new corporations that would concentrate economic and political power in potentially unaccountable institutions. In fact, Thomas Jefferson's vision for a Bill of Rights included "freedom from monopolies in commerce," except it wasn't incorporated into the final version, which was ratified on December 15, 1791.

Throughout the early 1800s, corporations were generally constrained to act within reasonable civic boundaries. But as industrialization gained pace, a great deal of capital was needed, so many more companies were formed to facilitate business activity: railroads, banks, and steel producers. Corporations took off, growing significantly in size, number, and influence.

In a letter to Col. William F. Elkins during the Civil War, dated November 21, 1864, President Abraham Lincoln warned of the dangers ahead:

> We may congratulate ourselves that this cruel war is nearing its end, but I see in the near future a crisis approaching that unnerves me and causes me to tremble for the safety of my country. As a result of the war, corporations have been enthroned and an era of corruption in high places will follow, and the money powers of the country will endeavor to prolong its reign by working upon the prejudices of the people until all wealth is aggregated in the hands of a few and the Republic is destroyed. I feel at this moment more anxiety for the safety of my country than ever before, even in the midst of war.

After the Civil War, the 14th Amendment was passed in 1868 to protect the rights of the freed slaves. It was the most important constitutional change in the country's history since the Bill of Rights, extending "equal protection" to all American citizens: "No state can deprive any person of life, liberty, or property without due process of law."

Years later, in 1881, California imposed a special tax on railroad property, and the Southern Pacific Railroad Company pushed back with a bold case to be treated under the law as a legal "person," reasoning that just as the 14th Amendment bars discrimination based on racial identity, so does it bar discrimination based on corporate identity. The team of lawyers was led by Roscoe Conkling, a former leader of the Republican Party in Congress who served on the committee that drafted the amendment. The Supreme Court went along with it, and the decision was subsequently used as precedent to grant constitutional protections to corporations. And thus, constraints that had historically been placed on the corporate form were removed, and corporations obtained many of the same legal rights as persons: to own property, borrow money, and buy and sell goods in their own right.

Slavery was the legal fiction that a person is property, and corporate personhood became the legal fiction that a corporation is a person. By 1912, the Supreme Court read the 14th Amendment on twenty-eight cases involving the rights of African Americans and an astonishing 312 cases on the rights of corporations.

Mark Twain dubbed the decades after the Civil War the "Gilded Age"— an era of rapid industrialization and growth of America's first giant companies, but also an age characterized by corruption, materialism, and growing inequality. More and more wealth was concentrated in the hands of fewer people. By 1890, the richest 1% of Americans owned more property than the remaining 99% and received the same total income as the bottom half of the population. Two of the most well-known corporations were Andrew Carnegie's steel company and the Standard Oil Company, founded by John D. Rockefeller.

According to historian Eric Foner, one of the leading causes of the shift of American values and the destruction of the American dream was the rise of corporations:

> Americans found themselves at odds as they grew in awe, admiration, and hostility. Corporate leaders such as Carnegie and Rockefeller were considered robber barons who wielded power without any accountability in an unregulated marketplace. Mostly hated for their domineering positions, repressive mentalities toward laborers, and display of selfishness, corporations were thought to undermine the ideas of political and economic freedoms as fair competition was altogether shattered in the face of monopolies.

The control of corporations over the political and economic realms of society was so vast that President Woodrow Wilson (1913–1921) describes, "a very different America from the old... no longer a scene of individual enterprise, individual opportunity, and individual achievement," but a country in which "comparatively small groups of men," corporate owners, "wield a power and control over the wealth and the business operations of the country," becoming "rivals of the government itself." Both Republicans and Democrats were not willing to sour relations with Big Business, though.

In the 1960s and 1970s, corporate America was further mobilized by Milton Friedman and his "Chicago School" economists promoting ultra-free-market capitalism based on neoliberal ideas of deregulation and privatization. In his book *Capital and Freedom*, Friedman writes, "There is one and only one social responsibility of business—to use its resources and engage in activities designed to increase its profits." The sole mission of business became "profit maximization." Economic efficiency and productivity was elevated over human dignity. Naomi Klein, an author and social activist, describes the neoliberal set of ideas as "a rationale for greed."

The inequality gap grew faster, but it was determined that it had to get worse before it could get better and that more growth would make it better. This was known as the "Kuznets Curve," resembling an upside-down "U"—inequality first rises, then levels off, and ultimately starts to fall. Even though the economist Simon Kuznets said that his work was 5% empirical and 95% speculation and "some of it possibly tainted by wishful thinking," this became the most widely accepted justification for trickle-down economics.

But as Thomas Piketty more recently points out in his book *Capital in the Twenty-First Century*, the level of inequality in America is "higher than in any other society at any time in the past, anywhere in the world." He argues that there is no reason to believe that capitalism can ever solve the problem of inequality, which is largely a corporate phenomenon. In the early 1980s, large American corporations still sent less than half their earnings to shareholders, spending the rest on their employees and other priorities. But between 2007 and 2016, they dedicated 93% of their earnings to shareholders, a very narrow class of people.

If corporations are legally classified as "persons," it begs a question: "What kind of person is the corporation?" Measured against moral people, philosopher Tim Dean argues that many corporations seem like psychopaths.

For a start, corporations feel no empathy, guilt, or remorse. And many corporations are explicitly established to generate a profit, so we know they primarily serve interests other than ours. What, then, do we make of a corporation that does things we consider bad, even if they're legal, such as selling a product it knows is both addictive and deadly; retrenching loyal staff and outsourcing to countries with far lower labor standards; or cutting costs by lowering safety rules to the absolute minimum that the law allows? If corporations are to be judged in the same way as people, perhaps many of them really are psychopathic.

In recent years, corporations have won more liberty rights, such as freedom of speech, religious liberty, and virtually unrestricted political contributions. "This is a Corporate Coup d'État," says Klein. If you think the present situation cannot be sustained for much longer, then think again. The long arc of history is clear: those who stand to thwart the corporate juggernaut are trampled by well-funded and powerful business elites.

> *To what purpose is all the toil and bustle of this world? What is the end of avarice and ambition, of the pursuit of wealth, of power, and preeminence?*
> — Adam Smith

The Feast

Chapter 5 in the Book of Daniel tells the story of King Belshazzar's feast. The Babylonian king holds a great banquet for a thousand of his nobles and orders that the gold goblets looted in the destruction of the First Temple in Jerusalem be brought in so that the revelers can drink from them. And so late into the night they drink wine and praise the gods of gold and silver, of bronze, iron, wood and stone.

Suddenly, a hand appears and writes on the wall: "mene, mene, tekel, upharsin." The frightened Belshazzar calls for the wise men of Babylon to interpret the writing, "Whoever reads this and tells me what it means will be clothed in purple and have a gold chain placed around his neck." But no one was able to read the writing. The diviners, enchanters, astrologers, and magicians—all were baffled, and the king became even more terrified.

The queen advises Belshazzar to send for Daniel, who is renowned for his wisdom. The king says to him, "Are you Daniel, one of the exiles my father brought from Judah? I have heard the spirit of the gods is in you and that you have insight, intelligence and outstanding wisdom. If you can read the writing on the wall and tell me what it means, you will be made the third highest ruler in the kingdom."

Daniel declines the king's offer of gifts and reminds him that God gave his father, Nebuchadnezzar, sovereignty and greatness, but when he became arrogant and his heart filled with pride, he was deposed from his royal throne and stripped of his glory. He suffered a humiliating period of madness until he learned that God is sovereign over all kingdoms on earth and sets over them anyone he wishes.

"But you, Belshazzar, his son, have not humbled yourself, though you knew all this," Daniel answers. "You have desecrated the treasure taken from the temple and honored the gods which cannot see or hear or understand. You have set yourself up against our Grand Creator, who has given you all this splendor. That is why God has sent the hand to write these words."

Daniel then reads the message: "God has numbered the days of your reign and brought it to an end. You have been weighed on the scales and found wanting. Your kingdom is divided and given to the Medes and Persians." Even while Daniel is speaking, the Medes and the Persians have begun to attack Babylon. That very night, Belshazzar, the king of Babylon, was slain, and Darius the Mede received the kingdom.

May that Almighty Hand guide and uphold us all.

> *Bow your head further down (in humility)*
> *Fakir, bow your head further down*
> *There is great pleasure in holding the head high (in arrogance)*
> *But, that pleasure will never be fulfilling*
> *Bow your head even further down*
> *One day you will be bestowed with His presence*
> *Fakir, bow your head further down*
> *Bow your head further down*
> — Shah Hussain

DAMN

> *We're in a time where we exclude one major*
> *component out of this whole thing called life: God.*
> — Kendrick Lamar Duckworth

Kendrick Lamar is the greatest rapper of our time. He has been described as the "poet laureate of hip-hop," whose technical gift for putting words together has been compared with James Joyce and James Baldwin. Three times he was nominated for the best-album Grammy and didn't win, but he did win the Pulitzer Prize for his fourth album *DAMN*—the first nonjazz or classical artist to collect that honor in its seventy-five-year existence.

Born and raised in Compton, California, it is Kendrick's honest introspection in verse about being young, black, poor, and gifted in America and the clarity and lyrical deftness with which he describes his true feelings, his emotions, the pointed social commentary, and a breakdown of cultural barriers that have made him sublime.

For example, on racial tensions, he strikes: "We look so much on color that we forget about the soul." On the violence that ravages society: "The one in front of the gun lives forever." On making a difference: "I can't change the world until I change myself first." Focusing on the self: "Don't you know your imperfections is a blessing." On love: "Love is not just a verb. It's you, looking in the mirror." And on religion, he reminds us: "We're all put on this earth to walk in His image, the Master."

From thirteen years of age, Kendrick was in a curious mode of mastering how to be a rapper, calling himself K-Dot, using his tongue as a sword, slaying words. "When I stopped going by K-Dot, that was the moment where I really found my voice," Kendrick remembers.

When he turned twenty-two, he started developing and actually constructing music from a writer's point of view. "Since the first time I touched the pen, I wanted to be the best at what I do." He added, "I just love words. I love how to bend them, I love how to break them, I love how to twist them, turn them, make them couplets. That shows the true craft." His second album *Good kid, M.A.A.d City* could actually be unfolded into a book and read.

His creative process starts with a whole bunch of premeditated thoughts. Kendrick thinks about the ideas and what he wants to say next. He lives with the concept and makes notes. His greatest skill is taking cohesive ideas and turning them into gripping storytelling: "This is more than just music for me. This is actually a piece of me. I'm obsessed with it." Then, in the studio, he figures out the sounds, how to attack the track, and constructs all the pieces together. "Execution is my favorite word," he states. "I spend 80% of my time thinking about how I'm going to execute."

When Kendrick is completely drained of inspiration and starts to tamper with things that he shouldn't tamper with, that's when he knows he's finished with the project. That comes with not wanting to actually rush the process. But also because he is his own toughest critic. He avoids reading reviews of his music. "I've learned that my mission statement is really self-expression," says Kendrick. "My whole thing is to inspire, to better people, to better myself forever in this thing that we call rap. God put something in my heart to get across and that's what I'm doing. All I am is just a vessel, doing His work."

Fans of all identities can find themselves in Kendrick's music. They pick apart every verse, rapping it lyric for lyric, bar for bar, pulsating to the beat, hands held aloft to punch through the sky as they sing along. "It's bigger than just my story," Kendrick realizes. "That always blew my mind."

> *Let yourself be silently drawn by the stronger pull of what you really love. It will not lead you astray.*
>
> — Rumi

Evolve

"There is no significant example in history before our time," the great historians Will and Ariel Durant note, "of a society successfully maintaining moral life without the aid of religion." Contrary to modern day pseudo-intellectuals, who regard religion as particularly violent and the source of great evil, the Durants' work finds that religion brings subtle and pervasive gifts to society. I quote from *The Lessons of History*, which is a condensed version of the couple's life's work:

> Even the skeptical historian develops a humble respect for religion, since he sees it functioning, and seemingly indispensable, in every land and age. To the unhappy, the suffering, the bereaved, the old, it has brought supernatural comforts valued by millions of souls as more precious than any natural aid. It has helped parents and teachers to discipline the young. It has conferred meaning and dignity upon the lowliest existence, and through its sacraments has made for stability by transforming human covenants into solemn relationships with God. It has kept the poor from murdering the rich. For since the natural inequality of men dooms many of us to poverty or defeat, some supernatural hope may be the sole alternative to despair. Destroy that hope, and class war is intensified.

We are living through unsettled times, and in the eyes of the Durants, the fact that nations have dispensed with theological foundations has a lot to do with it. The Industrial Revolution replaced religious traditions with secular institutions. The breakthroughs and triumphs of scientific technology succeeded the inculcation of a supernatural creed and moral code. So as science became the religion of the modern man, the West lost widespread religious practice. Modernity slowly weakened spirituality, and we collectively turned to commerce as our new way of worship—the ever-more efficient meeting of needs and wants. Today, we live in a culture increasingly devoid of faith. The white noise of capitalism and secularism has smothered it.

And so the burden of inequality and mental health conditions is on the rise. More than 300 million people of all ages suffer from depression worldwide, 767 million people live in poverty (or under $1.90 a day), and global hunger is affecting 800 million people. How is it that there is still so much suffering in this world in what we proudly call our age of abundance? About $30 billion is needed to feed the world's hungry, but Americans spend over $60 billion a year on weight loss programs and products. So there is enough capital to go around; it's just that our system is designed to maximize profit, not minimize human suffering.

According to Leo Tolstoy, the only real science is the knowledge of how a person should live his life. The Russian writer, who is regarded as one of the greatest authors of all time, believed that life should be directed by the spiritual element that is manifested in the heart of every individual and gives life to all that exists. He takes aim at the delusion and pride of our intellect:

> The term "scientific" is understood just what was formerly understood by the term "religious"—just as formerly everything called "religious" was held

> to be unquestionable simply because it was called religious, so now all that is called "scientific" is held to be unquestionable... The unfortunate majority of men bound to toil is so dazzled by the pomp with which these "scientific truths" are presented, that under this new influence it accepts these scientific stupidities for holy truth.

At a lunch table recently, I had the pleasure to be seated next to someone remarkable who has started to question this scientific rationalism: Bo Shao. Bo was born to a poor family in China. But he excelled in math, which earned him a scholarship to Harvard University. He returned home and started a tech company, which he sold to eBay four years later for a few hundred million dollars. He then cofounded Matrix Partners China, which is today one of the most successful venture funds in the world. But Bo said that, somehow, reaching the pinnacle of success proved less satisfying. He felt empty and reluctantly embarked on a journey to find ways to improve his life, learning from the teachings of the great saints and sages from both the East and the West.

"Accelerating technological development is intoxicating, but dangerous if it is not balanced by other areas of human development," Bo told me. "We understand so much about the external world, but still so little about ourselves."

Scientific progress has improved our living standards, but many people today feel lonely, unhappy, purposeless, fearful, or anxious. Everyone you meet is fighting a personal battle. Through his inner journey, Bo came to understand that self-discovery and realization hold the key to discovering joy, inner peace, and freedom.

He is now devoting his efforts toward a philanthropic endeavor to reduce suffering from issues internal to our soul, which, in turn, would help improve our external circumstances. He launched Evolve Foundation, giving $100 million to invest in companies dedicated to using technology to further develop and advance humanity's consciousness to maximize the social good.

Here's Bo talking about his newfound mission:

> Technology is a double-edge sword. It can be used to amplify our craving for more things, more stimulation, or to make us more present, more aware. There are a variety of tools that can help us do inner work. Some of them, such as meditation, yoga, and breathwork have ancient roots. Others, such as psychological or neurological based healing, are modern. Still others, such as mobile apps for meditation, use modern technology to augment ancient ones. Dharma (teachings), sangha (community), and teacher will all benefit from technology in ways that we cannot yet fully imagine.

Bo hopes that new solutions will emerge when we start by resolving the issues on the "inside" and put humanity in the center, re-examining how we have constructed our economic system and built businesses in relation to them. "It is possible to end our suffering if we work on our inner self," Bo said convincingly. "And when we end our own suffering, perhaps we can use our newfound freedom and wisdom to help others end theirs."

Something needs to be done for our spiritual malady—the threat it poses to our world is evident. It's time to evolve.

The Writing Life

My goal in life was to be a hedge fund manager. There was no way I wouldn't be managing other people's money by the time I turned thirty. This desire was born only a few months into my first job as a bank teller. So I spent the next few years readying myself. According to plan, I quit my job in the fall of 2012, aged twenty-eight, and went out to raise capital.

I looked at people like Stan Druckenmiller and Paul Tudor Jones. They kicked off their funds with about a $1 million. That is all I needed to build a track record. After a few good years, the world would find me in the sanctuary of my bedroom and spring me to stardom. Soon, I'd be running a billion dollars.

It took me a year to fix together $1.6 million from family and friends. But I wasn't as happy as I expected to be. In pitch meetings to prospective investors, my heart felt out of place. The fire inside had cooled down and in its place was conflict. It felt like I was cheating myself, which meant that I was also cheating the investor who trusts me with his savings.

"Is this not what I always wanted?" I asked myself in doubt.

The question called on me to figure out who I am. I didn't have the maturity or sensibility to realize at the time, but I had become a different person. I wasn't the same Jawad as the one who set the goal to be a hedge fund manager. Each day, we change, our experiences alter our perspectives, and over time, that multiples; yet I foolishly stuck to an ideal sucked in from the past.

I dropped the idea to launch a hedge fund, and for the first time in my life, the wise guy in me had no plans.

Six months later, I started writing *Stray Reflections*. Though I shared it with friends and peers, I really was just writing for myself. As Henry Miller said, "Writing, like life itself, is a voyage of discovery." I was still without answers.

That should have been a clue—my choice for the name of the publication—that I'm drawn to the writing life. That is a truth which was not obvious to me at the time. I think it is because I had not fully given up on the hedge fund persona, clinging to it as my only sense of self-worth. Besides, I found it incredibly hard to write. Shouldn't doing what you love make it feel easy?

Yet somehow, I've kept at it doggedly, more pleased and fulfilled than the old Jawad could ever have imagined. That is another sign to which I have only now awoken. As Steven Pressfield wrote in *The War of Art*, "The more important a call or action is to our soul's evolution, the more Resistance we will feel toward pursuing it."

Each day, I'm prepared to confront my own self-sabotage and sit down to write. As Jane Hirshfield is known to have once said, the work of writing is no "arbitrary tinkering" but a continued "honing of the self at the deepest level." But now that I realize this change in me, being drawn to the writing life more than the investing life, I'm confronted with another question: Am I still qualified to provide investment advice? The question frightens me.

Good writing, like investing, is about seeking the truth. So I write to learn. When I'm writing, the doors of perception open. I'm constantly refining and redefining my own perspective as I try to find my way through a maze. The writing process reveals what is interesting and what is not and, by extension, what I'm supposed to be writing. That is a great responsibility. I myself like or dislike writers mainly for what they choose to show or make me think about.

When asked "What is the goal of a writer?" Anne Lamott responded, "I think, to help others have this sense of wonder, of seeing things anew, things that can catch us off guard, that break in on our small, bordered worlds."

Should I be anything else?

> *There is nothing to writing. All you do is sit down at a typewriter and bleed.*
> — Ernest Hemingway

Deep Work

I'm not a natural writer. Each month, I struggle to get going. There is a distinct feeling of strain as I stare at the blank white screen. The pressure slowly builds up, and when I feel I can wring something, anything that has matured in my mind, I write it down—in spurts. I'm painfully picky about the placement of words.

Poring over the writing rituals and routines of celebrated authors helped me realize that I'm not alone in my suffering. "I have to write hundreds of pages before I get to page one," confessed Barbara Kingsolver. "Laborious" and "disappointing" is how Khaled Hosseni described his first drafts. But the great Maya Angelou said it best, "Easy reading is damn hard writing."

I thought that as the years go by, the process would get easier, but I have not been so lucky. If anything, in a world full of digital diversions, it has only become more difficult to maintain a state of unbroken concentration and produce in terms of both quality and speed. This is why deep work—the ability to work for an extended period of time on a cognitively demanding task free from distraction—is so important to produce at our highest level. Author Cal Newport calls deep work, "the superpower of the twenty-first century."

I used to blame time and complain that there's just not enough of it. But the truth is that most of our time management issues are really just attention management issues. Oftentimes, I decide midsentence that it's more important to put some music on, check my Twitter feed, or research some question online. Novelist Don DeLillo describes this: "A writer takes earnest measures to secure his solitude and then finds endless ways to squander it."

When we switch between tasks, our attention doesn't immediately follow. A residue of our attention remains stuck thinking about the original task. This residue gets especially thick if our attention remains divided for a while, which leads to poor performance. This should be self-evident, but in our increasingly complex and competitive information age, nothing is obvious until it is pointed out.

According to Newport, "The key to developing a deep work habit is to move beyond good intentions and add routines and rituals designed to minimize the amount of your limited will power necessary to generate meaning in the daily efforts of your professional life." To focus on being present and productive instead of just busy, I now carefully build my days to contain and control the chaos of everyday life.

What I have worked out is this: I wake up at quarter past five, pray and worship in the morning, which I have all to myself. Then, I take a cold shower at half past seven, which makes me feel alert and energized. By this time, the rest of the household is waking up, so we have breakfast together. At nine o'clock, I head to my office, which is at home. To make deep work possible, I leave my phone behind and switch off the Internet to create an environment that allows for concentrated absorption. This won't necessarily make me a better writer—words don't come easy to me—but the importance of putting my backside in the chair day after day and focusing intensely on a specific deep work task is no longer lost on me.

At one, I stop work and pick up my daughter from school. Lunch is at home, and I go back to work at three and continue uninterrupted until five. The next three hours, I devote time to my family. I play with my children, spend time with my wife, have dinner, and help with bedtime. At eight, when the house is getting quieter and my productivity level is lower, I batch the shallow activities I cannot avoid into smaller bursts. So if I've got emails to write or need to take calls, I block off some time to just focus on those tasks. I would like to shut down considering work issues completely, but this is still difficult. I'm always going to be a work in progress. But I work no later than ten, when I put away my phone and laptop, finish my prayers, and wind down to sleep. If I go to bed any later than eleven, I have trouble waking up on time in the morning. Your day starts when you go to sleep.

"A schedule defends from chaos and whim," wrote Annie Dillard. "It is a net for catching days." The purpose of routine is to bring order and discipline and to fall in love with ritual and repetition. The perfect life starts with the perfect day, which is maybe all we have.

> *We are what we repeatedly do. Excellence, then, is not an act, but a habit.*
>
> — Aristotle

The Unknown

One time, film director Alfred Hitchcock was working on a problem he was having with a scene. There were a lot of things to consider—lighting, staging, pacing, and the like. He was up late with actor Hume Cronyn and his team struggling to find the right way to do it. Finally, when they seemed close to the solution, Hitchcock started telling jokes and got everyone off track again. Later, Cronyn asked him why he chose to do that when they were so close to solving the problem. Hitchcock paused before saying, "You were pushing. It never comes from pushing."

When it comes to certain complex problems, we find ourselves continually caught in this loop of trying so hard that we stymie our own efforts. Many people will not tolerate a state of doubt, either because of the mental discomfort or because they regard it as evidence of inferiority. However, to be genuinely thoughtful, we must surrender to not knowing the solution and be willing to sustain and protract that state of doubt. The most important things show themselves slowly, and they do so in their own time.

A growing literature in the psychology of perception has come to support Hitchcock's actions. When a difficulty stimulates the mind, simply relaxing and letting the answer "pop out" works much better than actively trying. It is said Edward Gibbon conceived his magnus opus, The History of the Decline and Fall of the Roman Empire, while listening to a choir of monks at vespers. Nobel physicist Steven Weinberg was nagged by the problem of how nuclear reactions produce the heat of the sun—until it came to him one day unbidden as he was driving. Allegedly, Archimedes discovered the law of specific gravity while taking a bath. To quote author Wayne Muller, "Sometimes our greatest wisdom comes when we are not striving to discover anything at all." Goethe said that we will always be making mistakes as long as we are striving after something.

When we let the problem alone, when we embrace the unknown and let the subconscious mind take over, then it has the space it needs to solve the problem itself. It's only by having some distance from the problem that we can see it as a whole and understand what we should be doing with it. Somehow, we have to combine relaxation with activity. Aldous Huxley puts it elegantly:

> In all the activities of life, from the simplest physical activities to the highest intellectual and spiritual activities, our whole effort must be to get out of our own light... what has to be relaxed is the personal self, the self that tries too hard, that thinks it knows what is what, that uses language. This has to be relaxed in order that the multiple powers at work within the deeper and wider self may come through and function as they should. In all psychophysical skills we have this curious fact of the law of reversed effort: the harder we try, the worse we do the thing.

Whenever Albert Einstein was stuck on a problem, he would often take refuge in music, and that would usually resolve his difficulties. After playing, he would get up from his piano saying, "There, now I've got it!" It is not well known but Einstein, one of history's most celebrated physicists, was a gifted musician. He attributed some of his greatest scientific breakthroughs to his violin-playing breaks, rather than any talent for absorbing absolute knowledge.

"If I were not a physicist," he once said, "I would be a musician. I often think in music. I live my daydreams in music. I see my life in terms of music. I get most joy in life out of music." Something in the music would guide his thoughts in new and creative directions. "Combinatory play seems to be the essential feature in productive thought," Einstein alleged. This allowed him to develop parts of his brain in new ways, and discover connections that, even if obvious, seem to escape detection.

Einstein believed that there comes a point in everyone's life where only intuition can make the leap ahead, without ever knowing precisely how. "The intuitive mind is a sacred gift and the rational mind is a faithful servant. We have created a society that honors the servant and has forgotten the gift." He admitted that the theory of relativity occurred to him by intuition, and that music was the driving force behind this intuition. "My new discovery is the result of musical perception," he said. Einstein rarely left home without his beloved violin, Lina.

My choice of play is poetry, which stimulates the right hemisphere of the brain, the same as music. I like to approach the world of global macro investing like a poet contemplating an epic in progress—conjuring up battles in our imagination, inventing and discarding subplots, balancing rhyme and reason. When feeling totally lost about something, I disappear into the garden to read a few verses. Researchers have shown contemplating poetic imagery and the multiple layers of meanings in poems activate specific areas of the brain that help us peer into the unknown and interpret our everyday reality.

When I find a pattern or connect countless dots to form a particulate cloud of ideas, I come back and jot something down. Somehow, unrelated facts can all be then thematically organized into coherent theories. Like Einstein, there are times when I feel certain I am right, without ever knowing the reason. And like Einstein, I have no special talents. I am only passionately curious.

> *I am the wisest man alive, for I know one thing, and that is that I know nothing.*
>
> — Socrates

The Walk

> *Walking is falling forward. Each step we take is an arrested plunge, a collapse averted, a disaster braked. In this way, to walk becomes an act of faith. We perform it daily: a two-beat miracle—an iambic teetering, a holding on and letting go. For the next seven years I will plummet across the world.*
> — Paul Salopek

Five years ago, two-time Pulitzer Prize–winning journalist Paul Salopek set out on a walk to rediscover the world. He took his first step in Ethiopia's Great Rift Valley, and his 21,000-mile trek will take him from East Africa north into the Levant, across the desert expanses of the Arabian Peninsula, through Asia, and then by sea from Siberia to Alaska, and down the western edge of the Americas to the southern tip of Chile. His storytelling project, entitled "Out of Eden Walk," traces the footsteps of our forebears and is an immersive global mosaic of human life.

"The world isn't flat. It's deeply corrugated, and some of the best stories lie in the hidden corrugations." Inspired by this belief, Paul chronicles his slow journey and the lives of people encountered on his journey: the villagers, nomads, traders, farmers, soldiers, and artists who rarely make the scoop. He hopes this gives readers at least one small outlet to a wider horizon and maybe even empathy for "The Other." It is about seeing ourselves in each other.

"I travel to and from *people*," he told the *National Geographic*. "People are both my refuge and my destination... This project isn't so much a long walk as a decade-long conversation at a rather large dinner table called Earth, with a rotating cast of hosts."

Paul, who is now 56, has logged over 10 million footsteps, and he is still not even halfway through his stroll. He is in India at the time of writing this and will traverse the green pathways of Bangladesh next, onward to the edge of China.

The world is growing complicated. And the explosion of information is almost unprocessable and only muddles our understanding. What we need is more "meaning," which can only be attained by slowing down and observing the world carefully. Paul's quest on foot is just one example of trying to tackle this challenge. By moving at a distinctly human pace of 5 km an hour, instead of crisscrossing maps by jet and car, he aims to deepen our perspective by *walking through* the major stories that are defining our age, such as climate change, conflict, poverty, mass migration, and technological revolution. The "Out of Eden Walk" is basically experiencing the news as a form of pilgrimage.

In January 2013, Paul kicked off his boot-level project from the Afar region of northeastern Ethiopia. He writes:

> How best to glimpse an individual's core values at the start of the twenty-first century? Look down at their feet—not into their eyes. Footwear is a hallmark of modern identity. In the affluent global north, where fashion caters to every whim and vanity, shoes announce their wearer's class, hipness, career choice, sexual availability, even politics (the clog versus the cowboy boot). It is disorienting, then, to be walking through a place

> where human beings—millions upon millions of women, men, and children—slip on identical-style footwear every morning: the cheap, democratic, versatile, plastic sandal of Ethiopia. Poverty drives demand. The only brand is necessity.

Two weeks into his journey through the scorching deserts of Ethiopia on his way to Djibouti, Paul confronted his first and recurring challenge: water. He writes:

> The world changes when you are thirsty. It shrinks. It loses depth. The horizon draws close. The desert tightens around you like a noose. This is the thirsty brain compressing the distances of the Rift, sucking in the miles through the eyes, magnifying them, probing them for any hint of water. Little else matters.

And to think nearly one billion people do not have access to clean and safe drinking water. For more than three years on his trek, Paul struggled to find it.

Lost in the deserts of Jeddah, Saudi Arabia, in May 2013, he writes:

> Being a little lost is good, because it keeps you alert, keeps you looking around. It keeps you scanning the horizons about to find your bearings, and you are not sleepwalking through the world... The world's first walkers had no maps. The concept of "destination" had yet to be invented. Each virgin horizon

unfolded with an open-ended question:
Where next?

In a world where nearly one person is forcibly displaced every two seconds and with nearly twenty-five million refugees, over half of whom are under the age of eighteen, we are living through the greatest mass migration ever known. And as always, the final destination remains unclear.

Near Mursitpinar in Turkey, on September 2014, Paul shares his thoughts on the global refugee crisis:

> Walking out of Africa, I personally have encountered hundreds of homeless Syrians along the trail. They are everywhere. Some picked vegetables in Jordan for $11 a day. They begged on street corners in the Turkish port of Mersin, their children so filthy as to be untouchable. The officers aboard the old livestock boat that carried me across the Red Sea couldn't sail for home. They didn't have one: They were Syrians. There are about three million Syrians hunkered, simmering, homeless and unmoored from normal lives, from hope, across the Middle East. Probably more. Include the Iraqis shoved aside by spillover fighting, and the total number of destitute, uprooted people in the region now scrapes five million. If you think this exodus won't touch you, you are a fool. Your grandchildren will be grappling with the fallout from this calamity.

On a 1,500-mile walk along the famous Silk Road trade route in 2016, which is being revived under China's Belt and Road Initiative, Paul recalls a time when the world came together in Central Asia:

> The Silk Road trafficked more than luxury goods: silk, gold, porcelain, spices. It connected a hundred million lives across the Old World. It was a conduit for transformative ideas, for novel technologies. Greek philosophy seeped east, helping to foster an Islamic Golden Age of art and science. Eastern breakthroughs such as paper, forged steel, and high mathematics trickled west, helping to ignite the European Renaissance. Trade among civilizations broadened the human imagination. It cracked open the world. Yet others things traveled the Silk Road too. Nomad raiders. Wars. The ancient highways of commerce funneled the Mongol hordes. Then came the plague. Business wealth stoked polarization, dynastic struggles. Walls rose around minds as well as cities. Slowly, or almost overnight, the great multiethnic trading kingdoms of Asia devolved into paranoia, intolerance, tyranny, darkness.

This sounds eerily familiar to our generation's pioneering experiment in globalization. Ideas, money, and people move around the planet faster than ever before because of major advances in transportation and communications technology. Economic integration was seen as a positive force, lifting people out of poverty in much of the emerging world, with improvements in their standards of living and health conditions. But the contemporary lament of globalization is that the global elites grew increasingly distant from the needs at the ground level—wages stagnated for the vulnerable middle class in the rich world, and gains from market reforms went disproportionately to the top of the income distribution, stoking a populist resurgence. Airlines also carried terrorists and infectious diseases, and a multipolar world meant the rise of strongmen and more international conflicts.

Accordingly, the future is moving toward greater insecurity, trade barriers, closed borders, xenophobia, and capital controls. We are returning, once again, to the politics of paranoia, intolerance, tyranny, and darkness. Paul's account of the Silk Road reminds us that history does not always move forward. It's often the same old story. To quote George Santayana, "Those who do not remember the past are condemned to repeat it."

The "Out of Eden Walk" has been obstructed by the changing times: "These ethnic fault lines, these imaginary glacial walls called borders... they have knocked me sideways, way off my intended track. For borders rule the most powerful topography on the planet: the corrugations of the human mind." Paul has been looted, ambushed, nearly shot, and stopped by local security forces eighty-four times. He is behind on his schedule, but he is still determined to walk long enough to complete the project. "I'm having the time of my life." The quest demands patience, fortitude, and stillness.

From the Pamir Mountains of Tajikistan in August 2017, Paul thinks about the children he met along the way:

> I am walking across the world. And today,
> wherever I wander, it is often children who hail

me first. They wave from fields of ripe wheat in Turkey. Or grin from village doorways in Georgia. Or shout hello from a passing bus in Palestine. Once, two boys threw rocks at me from a hilltop in Jordan. It was a game. I was so far away as to not even be human. Yet with surprising frequency—in our age of fear and wariness of strangers—kids walk along with me through their small, busy little worlds, down their dusty streets, or across their lush green animal pastures, holding my dangling hand. The adults? They stiffen for a moment. Their brains work furiously. For an eye-blink, they pause to analyze our encounter for possible danger, for consequences, for embarrassments, before offering a greeting. But the kids—their eyes burn with raw curiosity. They brim with a thousand questions. Who as a child has not dreamed about walking away from home? To the farthest corner of the world? To the edge where the seas falls off? Children remember. Children understand.

"The way walking from Ethiopia to Pakistan has changed me is to reinforce my positivity, my sense of hope," Paul observes about himself as he crossed the wild Himalayan mountain frontier to arrive in northern Pakistan.

In May of 2018, he wrote:

> Walking the world is a dance. Take one step up a glacier: Slide back two. Cars treat you like

roadkill: Pirouette around them. Inch over a suspension bridge rocking high above a river in the Himalayas: Stretch out your arms like a flamenco aerialist. In this way, each footstep you place across the surface of the Earth becomes a choreography of anticipation. Your partner is landscape. She leads. You follow.

Spanning nations, continents, and time zones on foot—day after day, month after month—has altered the way I experience life on the planet. There is something about being simultaneously liberated and yet constrained by the space that your legs can caliper in a day that bestows an acceptance of reality, a sort of somatic equanimity. It's a tonic against hubris.

In more affluent and motorized countries, by contrast, people lose connection not only with their environment but with the shape of the world itself. Cars annihilate time and distance. Locked inside bubbles of metal and glass, confined to narrow strips of asphalt, we become drugged with speed, spatially retarded.

Joseph Campbell has particular relevance for Paul's heroic, against-all-odds kind of excursion. "The Hero's Journey" was his all-embracing metaphor for the deep transformation that heroes in every time and place seem to share. A call to adventure leads them from their known world into an unknown one, often introducing them to both wonders and dangers, discovering new powers or skills along the way. By the time the outward journey ends, the inner journey has left them forever changed. In Paul's case, more than 200,000 words of literary reportage, thousands of photos, and hours of video and audio recordings capture this transformation of both the outer and inner worlds. There are lessons in it for all of us.

"Questing... is not an ego trip," Campbell writes in *Pathways to Bliss*. "It is an adventure to bring into fulfillment your gift to the world, which is yourself... When we have truly given the gift of ourselves to the world—the fulfillment of that which is potential in each of us—we find ways to make a positive difference, and to inspire others to walk their hero's path."

Put your best feet forward.

Adventure is worthwhile.

—Aesop

The Concrete System

> "Natural beauty has a necessary place in the spiritual development of any individual or society... Whenever we destroy beauty or substitute something man-made and artificial for a natural feature of the earth, we have retarded some part of man's spiritual growth."
> — Rachel Carson

"Do you have rooms available?"

After three days traversing the mountainous valley in Hunza in the extreme northern part of Pakistan, we wanted a comfortable place to stay with warm running water and Wi-Fi. Luckily, we found this charming bed and breakfast, called Fallen Man's Heaven, in Gulmit and, tired and hungry, rushed inside.

"Yes, but I'm sorry, we only allow families."

The young woman was standing behind the counter in the kitchen, peeling onions. This was her private home.

"But we are a family," I said desperately and hugged my friend Pony.

"Nice try," she said, laughing.

"Please, just for one night. It's already 8 p.m. We'll be quiet and leave in the morning."

"Let me check with my husband. He'll be back soon. Why don't you tell me what you want to eat, and I'll cook dinner till then."

So there was a chance. No way they kick us out after feeding us, we said to each other. That violates all rules of the wonderful hospitality this region is renowned for.

"Can we please have the Wi-Fi password?"

Since we set off on our travel, we had no connection with the outside world. It was stressful just thinking about all of the emails and messages that must have piled up, waiting for our response. It was criminal to be unplugged for this long in our increasingly virtual, fast-paced life.

An attractive, rugged man with salt-and-pepper strands came through the front door and sat beside us on the wooden table. We all looked up from our screens.

"Welcome to our home. Where are you coming from?"

He introduced himself as Faiz. His wife, Saira, finished preparing a delightful feast. And we relaxed knowing we'd be able to stay for the night.

The next morning, we all slept in, and I spent thirty minutes on my phone before jumping out of bed, finally caught up with all the notifications.

The day was bright and clear, and Faiz was having tea on the deck. Behind him, the snow-covered mountaintops were ablaze with the glistening sun. He told us a story about his Snow Lake expedition, a high-altitude glacial basin in the Karakoram mountain range. It turned out that Faiz was an avid, professional high-end trekker with clients spread around the world looking to explore Pakistan's untouched marvels of nature.

We had come to Hunza with a similar purpose. But we weren't having the time of our lives. It took seven years to plan our friends' reunion, but we realized rather quickly that we were not ready for an adventure—neither physically nor mentally. It didn't help that we had an annoying guide who discouraged us every step of the way. We opened up to Faiz about our struggles as if he was our therapist.

"It's not your fault."

We all looked at each other, puzzled. For a moment, I even imagined the iconic Robin Williams scene from the film *Good Will Hunting*, in which he comforts Matt Damon's character using the exact same words.

"You've come from the concrete system. It will take some time for you to rediscover your true nature."

By "concrete system," Faiz meant our encased city life, trapped indoors, day in and day out. The result of mega cities and mass urbanization is that the average American spends 93% of his or her life indoors. Adults in the US spend less time outdoors than they do inside vehicles—less than 5% of their day. Worse, they spend over 10 hours a day in front of a digital screen. Time spent in parks, woods, or fields has shrunk dramatically because of the lack of green spaces, digital technology, and parents' safety fears. Three-quarters of UK children spend less time outside than prison inmates. A 2013 study found that four out of five children in the UK were not adequately "connected to nature."

Everything about the concrete system was unnatural—the food, music, even the people. Faiz and Saira, on the other hand, took pride in organic living. They built their cottage themselves over a period of several years and had their own little farm where fresh fruits and vegetables were handpicked every day. In the natural world, it seemed people could live happily without big houses and high-paying jobs. They spent less time working to earn money and more time doing the things that interested them.

"Life in the concrete system is very difficult," Faiz went on. "I know, I've lived there. The hustle bustle of the city not only kills our capacity for wildness and wonder, it destroys the human spirit. A little preparation can go a long way toward helping you endure in the natural world—and once you complete a trek, it will change the way you see everything."

Meeting Faiz smack in the middle of our trip seemed destiny. We no longer felt inadequate or out of place; we were encouraged to test the depths of our limits and the heights of our determination.

Coming into the trip, I was so arrogant about my abilities that I did not bring hiking boots, preferring to pack sandals and flat-soled Toms for comfort instead. Nature had taught me a lesson by not letting me near her. Following Faiz's advice, I borrowed old hiking boots, found a shrub to be my walking stick, and vowed to myself to keep standing and active during breaks (so the muscles remain energized and in motion) as opposed to just slumping on the ground.

The destination was Naltar, a lush valley at an altitude of 4,678 m. Nestled among giant mountain peaks and towering forest trees, Naltar hides seven magnificent lakes—each unique in its own beauty. Initially, the trek was fairly easy because of a gentle slope, but it got tougher as rain started to pour and the terrain steepened. I found myself looking at the ground and walking softly on the mountain soil, careful not to slip.

It took us eight hours to discover each of the lakes—and yet it felt like a breeze. We were filled with adrenaline and amazement. The Naltar trek had the most enchanting views I've ever seen.

And Faiz was right, the journey, undoubtedly one of the most enthralling experiences of my life, one steeped with awe and mystery, gave us new eyes with which to see everything. A lonely mountaintop, the stillness of a lake, or the winds of a forest all have things to teach us.

Standing tall in the mountain forest, I felt small, a tiny speck of a massive universe swirling around. It helps to think in those terms because when we do, all our troubles seem trivial in the long history of the earth. We are not so impatient once we get a bigger picture of what is going on.

In the concrete system, we are all trying hard to be somebody, but here, in companionship with the earth, I realized the secret of being nobody. By a reduced sense of self-importance relative to something larger and more powerful that we are connected to, you can't help but feel generous and want to improve the welfare of others. There is a sense of peace and calm in knowing that we can play a small part in the intricate cosmic dance that is life.

Emerson said that we must foray into nature to understand the "perpetual presence of the sublime." Surrounded by God's wonder and beauty, I found myself unwittingly bowing my head in humility to move forward, watchful as not to make any wrong movement or crush or disturb anything in the least. In the natural world, we must let each step determine the next. We did not always know where we were going. This is in contrast to our urban reality, where we plan our whole lives out.

I arrived at a new, profound understanding of what British environmentalist Michael McCarthy meant when he wrote:

> The natural world is not separate from us, it is part of us. It is as much a part of us as our capacity for language; we are bonded to it still, however hard it may be to perceive the union in the tumult of modern urban life. Yet the union can be found, the union of ourselves and nature, in the joy which nature can spark and fire in us.

Live in each season as it passes; breath the air, drink the drink, taste the fruit, and resign yourself to the influence of the earth.

— Henry David Thoreau

The Hikam

Some books never lose their relevancy, no matter how old. Ibn Ata'illah's *The Book of Aphorisms*, written in the thirteenth-century, stands out as such. The book is a collection of 261 Sufi aphorisms, designed as a manual for spiritual development. Ata'illah guides us through his reflections and deliberations on how to live both outwardly and inwardly.

It's been a long time since I read a book that I loved this much. I see myself returning to it ritually every year alongside Rainer Maria Rilke's *Letters to a Young Poet* (Stephen Mitchell translation) and Allama Iqbal's *Shikwa and Jawab-e-Shikwa* (Khushwant Singh translation). Here are some aphorisms that resonated with me:

> Bury your existence in the earth of obscurity,
> For whatever sprouts forth,
> Without having first been buried,
> Flowers imperfectly.

For a seed to grow as a tree, it has to first bury itself in the soil. From the ground of insignificance, it sprouts forth to become a tree of significance, which yields flower and fruit. Likewise, for us to achieve true success, we have to bury our inclination for significance and reputation. The humbler one becomes the loftier he grows, the more arrogant one becomes the lower he plummets. Success achieved without humility will be short-lived.

> How can extraordinary things happen to you,
> When you, for your part,

> Have yet to rip apart the
> ordinariness of your life?

In other words, only those who succeed in vanquishing their worldly desires can develop their self to an extraordinary realm. The Divine light cannot feel at home in a heart which is teeming with earthly preoccupations.

> If you are confronted with two alternatives,
> Opt for the more difficult choice.
> What looks easy and comfortable,
> May not be good in the long run.

On the face of it, the easier choice will be of lesser risk while the difficult one will be less appealing. If we opt for what appears more relaxing, we will weaken our power to prevail over challenging and more rewarding tasks in the future and eventually succumb to a reduced state.

> Let God's taking notice of you
> Outshine people's taking notice of you
> And contemplate His treatment of you
> To outshine their treatment of you

Praise from people is harmful to spiritual health in the long run as it will gradually take our focus away from God to people. We must reflect on the Divine beneficence and not be led by people's comments and opinions. We should not extol ourselves, but rather praise God, because everything that we can stake a claim to is from Him.

Entropy

> *We must all wage an intense, lifelong battle against the constant downward pull. If we relax, the bugs and weeds of negativity will move into the garden and take away everything of value.*
> — Jim Rohn

The second law of thermodynamics describes the nature of entropy—that everything tends toward chaos and disorder. We see it in our everyday lives. A hot coffee becomes cold. Dirt piles up on the streets. Solid wood burns and becomes ash. Businesses fail. Our bodies decay. On a long enough timeline, entropy always wins. Therefore, life is characterized by our ability to temporarily hold at bay the ravages of entropy.

Entropy is always increasing. Stated in another way, the availability of energy is always decreasing. To return a system to its orderly state, it takes more energy than that which was required for disorder to happen. Therefore, as Tony Robbins says, "Energy is not only the basis of our existence, it is the fuel that makes everything in our lives real and possible. The higher your energy level, the more efficient your body, the better you feel the more you will use your talent to produce outstanding results."

We start out hungry and ambitious, but as we age, we become comfortable and complacent. The relentless tug of entropy drains us. Our energy levels fall, and we lose our drive and motivation. Daily, successful people reload themselves with energy to reverse the decay, using physical and mental strategies such as a regular morning routine, healthy diet, exercise, and mindfulness practices to let go of negative emotions and cultivate a gratitude mindset.

If we feel lethargic and depleted, we can't do a great job with our children because they have far more energy than we do. Without the necessary effort and vigilance, a business stops growing and reaches the point of maximum entropy: bankruptcy. All relationships go through fun and excitement, but even lovers who are the most compatible cannot prevent periods of stagnation and boredom. We need to put in the time and energy to minimize entropy and create long-term joy and commitment.

If life seems to always get more difficult and complicated, now we know why. Energy flows through into all areas of our life. Maintaining our health, relationships, careers, skills, knowledge, societies, needs a never-ending effort, and this requires more and more energy. "Disorder is not a mistake; it is our default," according to Shane Parrish. "Order is always artificial and temporary. The existence of entropy is what keeps us on our toes. Truly understanding entropy leads to a radical change in the way we see the world, and ignorance of it is responsible for many of our biggest mistakes and failures."

In a 1974 lecture, Nobel Prize—winning scientist, Albert Claude, honors life, discussing what it means to be engaged in a great labor of love, expending energy to fight back the tide of entropy so that a higher consciousness has a chance to emerge:

> Life, this anti-entropy, ceaselessly reloaded with energy, is a climbing force, toward order amidst chaos, toward light, among the darkness of the indefinite, toward the mystic dream of Love. Such a Nature does not accept abdication, nor skepticism.

The Edge

One question that I have struggled with my whole career is, "What's your edge?" It's tough. What can I say that I actually believe in my heart of hearts to be true? Not for a lack of trying, but my search has remained elusive. To this day, there is no proprietary model or magical method I have come across that I could say with confidence gives me an unfair advantage over others. There's no special technique or trading approach.

I know I am not unique in what I *do*. The only thing that is unique is *me*. So how I have learned to respond usually is by citing how I'm different. I didn't study at an Ivy league school, wasn't trained by an investment bank, and never worked for a hedge fund. I started my career as a bank teller.

And so, for the longest time, I thought my unconventional background was a shortcoming. I felt awkward in front of clients. But through their support and encouragement over the years, I saw that my perceived weakness was actually my core strength because it has helped me view the world differently from the vast majority of Western-born-and-trained analysts. As one client said to me, "There is great power in humility."

I'm not alone. Some of the greatest writers of all time had talents that were at odds with their experience. Far from undermining their credibility, the feeling of being far away from the work they wanted to accomplish was an essential part of its very discovery. They looked more closely at the subject precisely because they were curious and unfamiliar with it.

Alden Nowlan's poem, *The Seasick Sailor and Others*, portrays this genius. Can you guess which artists he is referring to?

> The awkward young sailor who is always seasick
> Is the one who will write about ships.
> The young man whose soldiery consists in the delivery
> Of candy and cigarettes to the front
> Is the one who will write about war.
> The man who will never learn to drive a car
> And keeps going home to his mother
> Is the one who will write about the road.
> Stranger still, hardly anyone else will write so well
> About the sea or war or the road.
> And then there is the woman
> who has scarcely spoken to man except her brother
> and who works in a room no larger than a closet,
> she will write as well as anyone who has ever lived
> about vast open spaces and the desires of the flesh.
> And that other woman who will live with her sister and
> rarely leave her village, she will excel
> in portraying men and women in society.
> And that woman, in some ways the most wonderful of them all,
> who is afraid to go outdoors, who hides when someone knocks,
> she will write great poems about the universe inside her.

From the top to the bottom, you have Herman Melville, Ernest Hemingway, Jack Kerouac, Emily Bronte, Jane Austen, and Emily Dickinson.

Melville jumped ship because he could not stand life aboard a whaler. He wrote *Moby Dick*. Hemingway spent most of his days in wars away from the fighting; hence, he became one of the greatest wartime writers. Kerouac was famously nomadic but wrote *On The Road* at the home of his mother. Jane Austen became the revered chronicler of courtship, love, and marriage. But she remained single. Emily Bronte was happiest in her own company, but in *Wuthering Heights*, she paints a viciously brutal world that led the Victorian public to think that it had been written by a man. And what can we say of Emily Dickinson? By choosing to live life internally, her poetry unveiled the secrets of the universe.

Could this be where a sustainable edge comes from? To observe from an unbridgeable distance with a mind freed from all conditioning. I don't own any stock or bonds or any investments for that matter. Could it be my own exile offers a very particular way of looking at markets that no one else possesses and inadvertently bestows very precise insights?

To play on the words of the eminent Indian philosopher, J. Krishnamurti:

> *Edge* is something extraordinary
> That comes naturally when you are
> watching without motive,
> Without any kind of demand,
> Just to watch and see the beauty of
> A single star in the sky,
> Or watch a single tree in a field...
> Then, in that watching
> In that alertness,
> There is something that is beyond words,
> Beyond all measure.

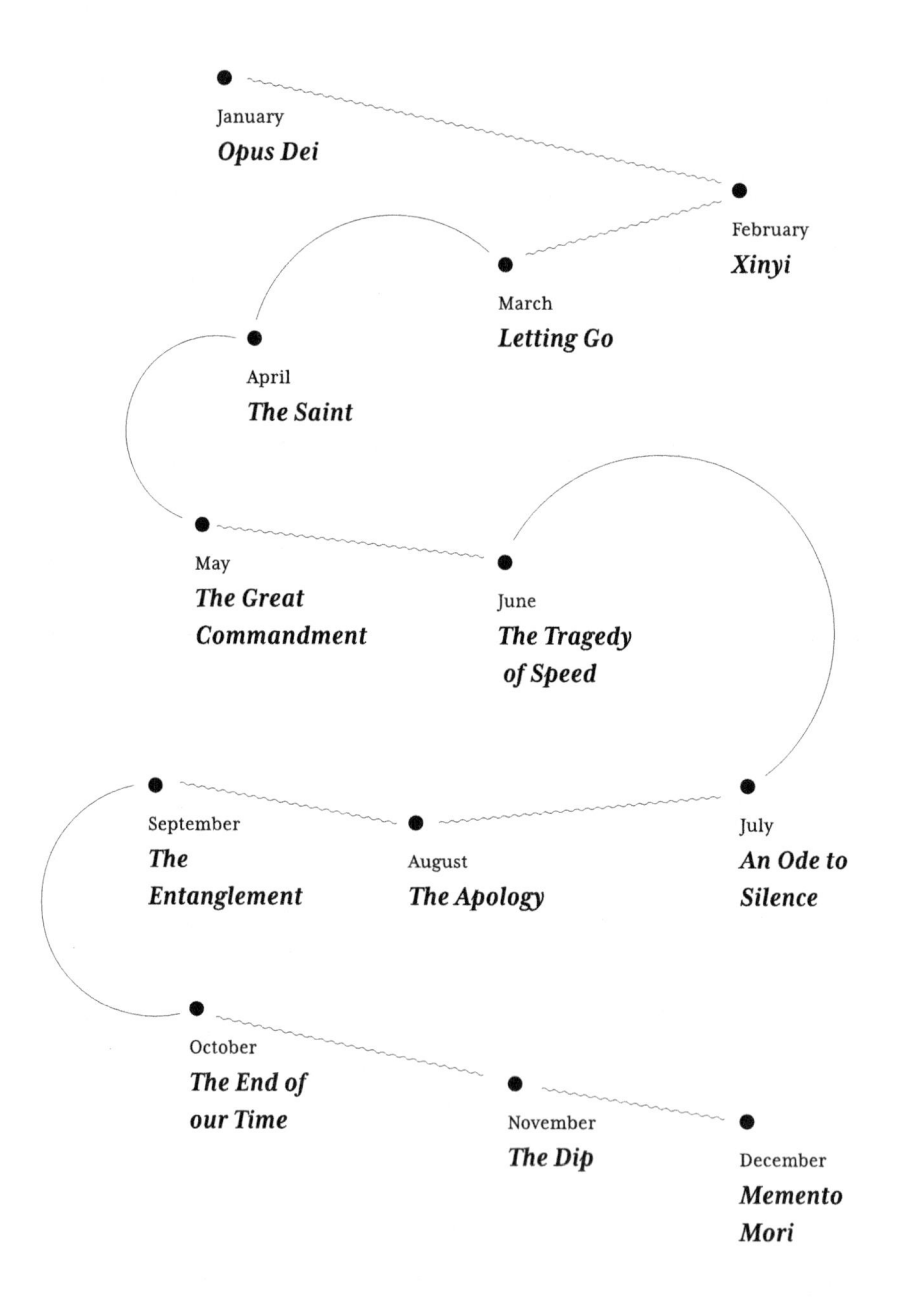

2019

January
Opus Dei

February
Xinyi

March
Letting Go

April
The Saint

May
The Great Commandment

June
The Tragedy of Speed

July
An Ode to Silence

August
The Apology

September
The Entanglement

October
The End of our Time

November
The Dip

December
Memento Mori

Opus Dei

"New Year, New Struggle." That was the motto Saint Josemaría Escriva set for himself on the first day of 1972. "This is our destiny on earth," he said to the people gathered at Roman College, "to struggle, for love." He alerted them to the need to begin again in the spiritual battle, reminding them of the words of Holy Scripture, "Is not man's life on earth just warfare?" We have to fight to overcome pride, greed, anger, lust, selfishness, and despair.

Inner peace is a consequence of war, of constant struggle. We are called to keep ourselves from being enslaved by sin and to infuse deep spirituality in every aspect of our lives so that we shall find peace. The fact is, as Escriva told them, life is a continuing process of starting over; one is always having to make acts of contrition, returning into God's arms, repentant, like the prodigal son: "You, my sons, will always struggle, and I too will try to always struggle, to the last moment of my life."

By striving to be holy in the ordinary circumstances of our lives—in one's time with family, during monotonous work, and even in interactions with complete strangers—Escriva believed that one's life could be sanctified. "We can all be saints in the world," he said. "A tailor saint, a baker saint, an office saint, a factory worker saint, a teacher saint." The observation of daily life is the greatest spiritual practice.

Xinyi

"Thank you," I said, jumping into my Uber ride, but it came out like I was pleading. "I'm late for dinner in Santa Barbara."

"Wait, what?" the driver looked back, confused. She tapped on her mobile screen and realized that I wasn't joking. From Santa Monica, which was where we were, to Santa Barbara was a two-hour-and-thirty-minute journey. It was peak rush hour.

Before she could change her mind—I could see the hesitation in her eyes—the cars behind honked, obliging her to flow into traffic. "This is the longest ride I've taken," she said as we got going.

I thanked her one more time. I told her I was only going for dinner and that, if she could wait, we could come back together. This relaxed her. As the sun set ahead, I relaxed myself as well, hoping to get some sleep. I was severely jet lagged.

"What does Jawad mean?" I opened my eyes, not knowing if I had rested for fifteen minutes or fifty.

"Well, it's an Arabic word which could mean a horse or someone who is generous. What about your name?"

"Xinyi means a joyous soul."

"Wow, that's beautiful," I said, suddenly feeling refreshed. "I love it."

Xinyi reached to her side and pulled out a notebook. She passed it back to me, "This is a gratitude journal. I request all passengers to spare a thought. It's anonymous, so you can have a read, and if you feel something, you can write too."

I flipped open the notebook and landed on a page that read, "Thankful to people that give others the benefit of doubt when conflicts happen." I thought of all the times I wrongly assumed the worst of someone. Here was a reminder to be patient in understanding.

This is such a great idea, I thought.

Xinyi told me she started gratitude journaling a few years ago when she was going through a rough time in her life. By practicing daily, she realized that it gradually changed the way she perceived situations by adjusting what she focused on. "Every day is a good day, at least in a small way." It helped her develop a positive frame of mind.

Then came the idea to start a journal for others to develop the habit. "The energy completely resets in the car." She was right. I felt calm and stillness as I peered out the window, reflecting on the things I'm thankful for.

"You have lived up to your name," I said.

The drive to Santa Barbara and back was special. Xinyi told me about her childhood in Heibi Province in China, the emotional torture she suffered at the hand of her sadistic parents, her escaping to America to study, the meditation retreat that saved her life, Buddhism, and the love she had of the great teachers from all traditions. Xinyi was only thirty-two, but she lived and traveled far, both inwardly and outwardly—and she cared so deeply to share her wisdom with me. It was the best car ride of my life.

Before I stepped out, I jotted down my thought in her gratitude book, as she requested. "Thankful to parents. Good or bad. We are a sum total of our experiences. We are who we are today because of them." I'll never be able to understand what Xinyi's been through, but I know that she would not be on this beautiful path otherwise—and this is what is most precious.

"Would you rather give this up in exchange for their love?" I asked, as she read my entry. It was her greatest longing.

She shook her head. "Why can't I have both?"

"Maybe because you will go on to relate to people and impact them in ways no one else can. Love can only be perfected in pain—and once perfected, lights other hearts."

A week later, Xinyi sent me a text, "I wanted you to know I've started a book for daily repentance. I've forgiven my parents for the way they treated me, but the memories burn in my heart still. I want to wash it away and live fully in the present. Thank you for encouraging me."

I wrote back, "I'm grateful to you and for you, Xinyi. Till we meet again."

Letting Go

> *When I let go of what I am,*
> *I become what I might be.*
> *When I let go of what I have,*
> *I receive what I need.*
> — Lao Tzu

Dr. David Hawkins is a world-renowned spiritual teacher and author of *Letting Go: The Pathway to Surrender*, published just before his death in 2012. Praised by Mother Teresa for his efforts to raise the consciousness of humankind, Dr. Hawkins shows readers how to rise up from those lower levels of emotional experience, such as shame, fear, greed, anger, and pride, into higher states of courage, acceptance, joy, and everlasting peace by just "letting go." Dr. Hawkins states:

> The average person is preoccupied with the body, its functioning, appearance, and survival. The average mind is beleaguered with worries, fears, and anxiety. With such inner tension, by the end of the day the average person frequently feels like a victim: drained, empty, and exhausted... Research has shown "letting go" to be more effective than many other approaches available in relieving the physiological response to stress. A feeling that is not resisted will disappear as the energy behind it dissipates. So as a person surrenders, it is accompanied by a feeling of relief and lightness, with happiness and freedom. There is a general reversal of pathological processes in

> the body and a return to optimal functioning.
> Physical and psychological disorders improve
> and frequently disappear altogether.

Letting go is incredibly difficult and is not the same as giving up. Letting go does not mean you stop caring either. It just means we cease our attempts to own and control the environment we are living in. Reaching greater clarity comes "not by finding the answers, but by undoing the basis of the problem," Dr. Hawkins writes. The basic idea is that when we are in a surrendered state, we are free of inner conflict and expectations. We let go of the attachment to our current experience of life and have no strong emotion about a thing: "It's okay if it happens, and it's okay if it doesn't." We develop an inner security, knowing that there will always be sufficient abundance. For me, that comes from my faith. Dr. Hawkins also states:

> When we are free, there is a letting go of attachments. We can enjoy a thing, but we don't need it for our happiness. Then, money becomes merely a tool to achieve our goals in the world... In the state of acceptance, there is the feeling that nothing needs to be changed. Everything is perfect and beautiful the way it is. There is a decreased preoccupation with "doing," and a growing focus on "being," which allows us to experience the basic nature of the universe, which, it will be discovered is to manifest the greatest good possible in a situation.

This is why "letting go" has frequently been called "getting present." In the process of letting go, we are no longer emotionally/psychologically invested in a "thing" (an idea, a goal, a position). As we learn to examine the feelings and ask from where they come, we can then let go of them. Thus, we regain our freedom, which also means we can be more present. And perhaps, we'll then notice the trees in winter, how they're experts at letting things go. To quote my friend Adam Robinson, "Each day presents us with 86,400 seconds, which means each day presents us with virtually countless opportunities to reset, recover our balance, and continue rehearsing our best selves."

This is the reality of it. And as it struck me a few years ago, my life has never been the same since.

> *We must be willing to let go of the life we've planned, so as to have the life that is waiting for us.*
>
> —Joseph Campbell

The Saint

What is the difference
Between your experience of Existence
And that of a saint?
The saint knows
That the spiritual path
Is a sublime chess game with God
And that the Beloved
Has just made such a Fantastic Move
That the saint is now continually
Tripping over Joy
And bursting out in Laughter
And saying, "I surrender!"
Whereas, my dear,
I am afraid you still think
You have a thousand serious moves.
— Hafiz

A young man went to a saint and said, "Teach me how to be successful."

"I will teach you more than that," replied the saint. "I shall teach you to be generous to the unsuccessful. That will pave the way toward your own success, and give you far more."

The young man was interested.

"I shall also teach you how to be generous toward the successful. Otherwise, you will become bitter and unable to work toward success."

"Please, tell me, how do I learn?"

"Seek first the kingdom of God, and all these things shall be granted to you," the saint said. "This sums up the teachings of the scriptures. The secret of all life is in these words."

The young man was confused. "But what about all my striving? There is so much I want to do, so much I want to achieve. I'm not ready to renounce the world."

The saint smiled. "Of course, you don't have to. That belief is an obstruction caused by our own misguided ego, which is the only thing we must renounce. What I mean to say is our work should be our religion, whatever our occupation may be. The purpose of one's life is to be a conscious instrument of the Divine Presence. The whole tragedy in the life of man is his ignorance of this fact."

The young man looked curious.

"There are two aspects of will working through all things in life. One is the individual will, and the other is the Divine will. When a person strives with all his might and yet finds difficulties all along the path and cannot achieve his desire, that is when the matter is contrary to the Divine will; naturally, his human will fails because he is swimming against the tide. The moment a person works in harmony with the Divine will, things become smooth."

"But how does one know the difference?"

"One feels that he is directing life or that life is happening to him. He is the doer. The other sees life happening for him and through him.

Whatever his life's pursuit, God is the doer, and he is His devotee."

"It's not that easy."

"It's not that difficult either. Listen to your heart. It knows all things."

"All my life I've been using my head."

"How's that working out for you?"

"Well," he fell silent.

The saint burst out laughing. "Try something different. Surrender."

The Great Commandment

> *You shall love your God with all your heart, with all your soul, and with all your mind. This is the first and great commandment. And the second is, you shall love your neighbor as yourself. On these two commandments hang all the law and the prophets.*
> — Matthew 22:37-40

"Excuse me, would you like a sandwich?"

So asks Austin Perine, a four-year-old boy dressed as a superhero, as he goes around the streets of Birmingham, Alabama to feed as many homeless people as possible. The caped crusader told his parents to take his allowance and money they would spend on toys to instead buy food for people who are hungry and who have no one to look after them.

When asked by a *CBS News* reporter why he does it, Austin politely replied, "You know what, Mr. Steve? It's just the right thing to do... Feeding the homeless is the highlight of my life." After Austin gives out the food, rising above the differences and distinctions that blind us, he also gives everyone the same piece of advice: "Don't forget to show love!"

At first, when I watched this news clip on Twitter, I thought it was cute. But then, as I watched the video again, his words, "Don't forget to show love," really stuck with me. I kept repeating it to myself over and over. It was a simple, yet powerful reminder from a four-year-old boy to always be kind and attentive. It was perhaps the best advice I have ever received.

What would it be like to be continually living with such overflowing love, reverence, and humility? To do something for the sake of its goodness, to selflessly put another person's needs before our own, without thought of any return whatsoever, and loving purely for the delight of loving?

Sheikh Sa'di said, "Higher spiritual life is nothing but service to humanity. It is not the rosary, or prayer carpet, or woolen robes." The greatest people in the world were all selfless in their devotion and duty.

We almost constantly think only about ourselves. And then, we get married and think about our spouse. Then, we have children and start to think about them. As our parents get older, we think more of them too. And when we have made "enough," we think of others out there.

But most of the time, if we are truthful, the things we do are all for ourselves, even though we like to believe they're not or that they may appear otherwise. Which is why Austin's message is so important. All of the strife and suffering of this world arise from not showing love.

> *In generosity and helping others, be like a river*
> *In compassion and grace, be like the sun*
> *In concealing other's faults, be like the night*
> *In anger and fury, be like the dead*
> *In modesty and humility, be like the earth*
> *In tolerance, be like the sea*
> *Either appear as you are, or be as you appear*
> — Rumi

"Don't forget to show love."

The Tragedy of Speed

> *There is nothing the busy man is less busied with than living. There is nothing that is harder to learn.*
> — Seneca

The volume of the work we must do divided by the time we have equals velocity. If our work keeps growing, but our time available stays the same or decreases, it increases the speed at which we have to work. Our culture pulls us into this orbit of speed. Speed gets noticed. Speed is praised by others. Speed makes us feel self-important.

But this acceleration is detrimental because not everything in life is moving at the same pace we are, and the faster we go, the harder it becomes to stop. In the ensuing exhaustion, we lash ourselves for not finding a proper work–life balance, for our inability to hold the competing parts of ourselves together in a more integrated and meaningful way.

In his book, *Crossing the Unknown Sea*, David Whyte speaks of the problem of speed:

> The great tragedy of speed as an answer to the complexities and responsibilities of existence is that very soon, we cannot recognize anything or anyone who is not traveling at the same velocity as we are. We see only those moving in the same whirling orbit and only those moving with the same urgency. Soon we begin to suffer a form of amnesia, caused by the blurred vision of velocity

itself, where those germane to our humanity are dropped from our minds one by one. We start to lose sight of any colleagues who are moving at a slower pace, and we start to lose sight of the bigger, slower cycles that underlie our work. We especially lose sight of the big, unfolding wave form passing through our lives that is indicative of our central character.

On the personal side, as slaves to speed, we start to lose sight of family members, especially children, or those who are ill or infirm, who are not flying through the world as quickly and determinedly as we are. Just as seriously, we begin to leave behind the parts of our own selves that limp a little, the vulnerabilities that actually give us color and character. We forget that our sanity is dependent on a relationship with longer, more patient cycles extending beyond the urgencies and madness of the office.

A friend falls sick, and in that busyness, we find their interruption of our frantic lives frustrating and distracting. On the surface we extend our sympathies, but underneath we are already moving in a direction that takes us far away. We flee the situation even if we are sending flowers every day; we rejoin, thankfully, the world that is on the go, on the move, untouched by mortality.

Once we ourselves are touched by that mortality,

however, through whatever agency it arrives in our lives a broken limb, the loss of a loved one, the collapse of our business, a moment of humiliation in the doorway of a meeting room our identities built on speed almost immediately fall apart and disintegrate. We find ourselves suddenly alone and friendless, strangers even to ourselves.

When it becomes all-consuming, speed is the ultimate defense, the antidote to stopping and really looking. If we really saw what we were doing and who we had become, we feel we might not survive the stopping and the accompanying self-appraisal. Speed is a sure sign that we are living someone else's life and doing someone else's work. But speed saves us the pain of all that stopping.

There is no hurry, and in a way, there is no future. It is all here—so take it easy, take your time, and get acquainted with it.
— Alan Watts

An Ode to Silence

> *Listen! Clam up your mouth and*
> *Be silent like an oyster shell,*
> *For that tongue of yours is*
> *The enemy of the soul, my friend.*
> — Rumi

On August 29, 1952, the piano virtuoso David Tudor walked onto the stage of the barn-like Maverick Concert Hall on the outskirts of Woodstock in New York. He sat at the piano, propped up six pages of blank sheet music, closed the keyboard lid, and clicked a stopwatch.

Thirty seconds passed. The audience, a broad cross-section of the city's classical musical community, waited for something to happen. Tudor turned one of the blank pages but made no sound. For four and a half minutes, he went about doing nothing. He never played a note. He then stood up, bowed, and walked off stage. That was all.

The piece was called "4'33," and it was composed by John Cage. Its purpose wasn't about listening to nothing. It was about listening to everything. "There's no such thing as silence," Cage said, recalling the performance. "You could hear the wind stirring outside, raindrops pattering the roof, and people themselves made all kinds of interesting sounds as they talked or walked out."

This was music for Cage, who socialized with Joseph Campbell and Alan Watts and became friends with Indian musician Gita Sarabhai, who taught him, "The purpose of music is to quiet and sober the mind, making it susceptible to Divine influences." Cage became concerned with silence, its nature, and how to engage it compositionally. His inventive compositions and contemplative writings, inspired by his interest in Eastern religions, influenced music for generations.

Given the iconoclastic nature of Tudor's performance at Maverick, there was, understandably, a certain amount of uproar. Even back then, sitting quietly for any length of time was not something people were accustomed to. "Silence was expelled," as the Swiss writer Max Picard observed in his profoundly illuminating book, *The World of Silence*. "It cannot be exploited for profit. It is unproductive. Therefore, it is regarded as useless."

This goes against the great wisdom of the ages, wherein silence is held as something that is sacred because it enables contemplation, introspection, meditation, and prayer. The ancient Greek philosopher Epictetus said, "Be silent for the most part." The aim might simply be of quiet submission, displaying humility and self-control, and renouncing our feeble efforts to comprehend the Divine.

Silence leads to stillness, and stillness leads to wisdom. When asked how to achieve enlightenment, a Zen master once gazed at the student with lips firmly sealed. When Buddha became enlightened, he kept silent. Words end where truth begins. The more we know, the quieter we become, and the quieter we become, the more we hear. "Silence is the root of everything," said Rumi. "If you spiral into its void, a hundred voices will thunder messages you long to hear."

The problem is that we live in an age of noise. Take a moment to think about the last time you could truly hear nothing. The space formerly occupied by silence is now full of clamor and abundance of activities, so much so that we don't even lament its absence; we are unaware that anything is missing. Of course, silence has not vanished: we have only lost touch with it.

"It is possible to reach silence anywhere," according to Norwegian explorer Erling Kagge, the first person to reach all three of the earth's poles on foot—the North Pole, the South Pole and the summit of Mount Everest. "I had to use my legs to go faraway in order to discover this. But I know silence can be anywhere, anytime—it's just in front of your nose." Kagge creates it for himself as he walks up the stairs, prepares food, or focuses on his breath. "You must create your own," he urges. "One only needs to subtract."

The word silence comes from the Latin word *silens*, which means to be still, to be quiet, or to be at rest. It is not merely an absence of external noise because silence speaks, within us and around us. It implores us to be more attentive to the world of which we are a part, to experience the fullness of time in the moment, and to humbly observe and process even our most uncomfortable thoughts. To quote John Cage, "We need not fear these silences, we may love them."

In his essay, "Return to Tipasa," the author Albert Camus describes a visit to ruins in Algeria—a place of great joy in his youth—in his search for renewed inspiration and sense of purpose:

> I listened to an almost forgotten sound within myself as if my heart, long stopped, were calmly beginning to beat again. And awake now, I recognized one by one the imperceptible sounds of which the silence was made up: the figured bass of the birds, the sea's faint, brief sighs at the foot of the rocks, the vibration of the trees, the

blind singing of the columns, the rustling of the wormwood plants, the furtive lizards. I heard that; I also listened to the happy torrents rising within me. It seemed to me that I had at last come to harbor, for a moment at least, and that henceforth that moment would be endless.

Silence is something that should be pursued, and the achievement of silence is something of which we should be proud.

All of humanity's problems stem from man's inability to sit quietly in a room alone.

— Blaise Pascal

The Apology

"What happened?" I ask, arriving at the scene of the fight.

"Zaynab kicked me!" It is my wife, Saniha, laying down the accusation. I glance over at my five-year-old daughter, who is standing beside her, unrepentant.

"She took my phone without permission and started watching videos. Twice, I asked her politely to give it back, but she completely ignored me. Then, I warned her a third time and snatched it because she didn't listen."

Saniha is feeling the side of her belly where it hurts. She looks like Winnie the Pooh at thirty-six-weeks pregnant.

"Say sorry to your mother." I want to defuse the tension.

Zaynab just stares at me. I look into her big brown eyes to glean if she feels any remorse. "Zaynab!" I insist, an edge of warning in my voice. Her face twists into a frown. She reminds me of how much you can articulate without words. As Susan Sontag said, "Silence remains, inescapably, a form of speech."

As the minutes pass, I feel myself getting angry. This is not the first time this has happened. I grab Zaynab forcefully by the arm and sit her down on the couch. "Is this how we behave? You need to say sorry now."

As parents, we want our children to take responsibility for their actions, consider others' feelings, and learn how to make up for their misdeeds.

One of our biggest challenges with Zaynab is that she refuses to apologize for anything. It's like her pride gets in the way. Rather than admit her fault, she deflects blame or acts in ways that are hurtful.

Saniha has been brought to tears several times. Among the things Zaynab has said to her: "You're just like Cinderella's wicked stepmother!" "I hate you, get out of my life!" and "I'm going to tell Baba to replace you with a new mother."

I look disappointingly at Zaynab. She is quiet for what feels like the longest time, her silence causing the anxiety in my chest to grow. I start to worry about her future. Novelist Emily Bronte's words echo in my mind: "Proud people breed sad sorrows for themselves."

In a flash, I picture Zaynab fighting with her husband, her inability to say sorry putting a strain on their relationship. I remember writer John Ruskin's advice: "It is better to lose your pride with someone you love rather than to lose that someone you love with your useless pride."

Pooh Bear mumbles something to herself and walks out of the room. It could be that her tummy is rumbling. Work beckons me, and I leave too, without saying another word.

Zaynab sits there, abandoned.

An hour later, Saniha comes into my office with a hand-written note.

> I want too apologis itz gist too hard.
> I wont to apolagis, I cant spel the rit werds out.
> Plees buleev me. I beg plees.
> I love you.

My heart sinks. I feel terribly ashamed for what I have done. I misunderstood Zaynab's silence to mean she was not remorseful, when, in fact, she felt bad about her actions and knew that she was in the wrong. She was just caught in a storm inside her.

What I realize in that moment is that Zaynab has trouble separating her actions from her character. If she does something bad, her mind makes her think she must be a bad person, which of course she is not. That is why admitting wrongdoing is difficult. Refusing to apologize was her trying to protect her fragile sense of self. Her pride serves as a defense mechanism.

What matters in how children turn out is how we turn out as parents. Rather than helping her communicate her genuine expressions, my actions were causing her to feel more humiliation. My eyes tear up.

As I walk back into the house, Zaynab stops playing with her toys and runs to me excitedly. I kneel down to receive her as she rushes into my arms with greater force than ever before. I regain my balance and squeeze her tightly.

"Baba, I wrote a letter and gave it to Mama, and we are now friends again. I said sorry and hugged her and…" Zaynab speaks in bursts of bubbly energy, a beautiful smile stretching across her face. She has completely forgotten my harsh treatment.

"Zaynab," I interrupt. "Will you forgive me?"

The Entanglement

Whoever finds love beneath hurt and grief
Disappears into emptiness
With a thousand new disguises
What is the soul?
What is the soul I cannot stop asking
If I could taste one sip of an answer
I could break out of this prison for drunks
I didn't come here of my own accord
And I can't leave that way
Whoever brought me here
Will have to take me home
— Rumi

According to data from the Centers for Disease Control and Prevention, suicide rates in the US increased by 30% between 2000 and 2016. Depression, drug and alcohol abuse, social isolation, financial setbacks, and relationship problems all have contributed to the rising suicide rates—the tenth leading cause of death in the US and one of three that is still increasing. In 2016, there were more than twice as many suicides as homicides, and it was the second leading cause of death for young people. What surprised the experts most of all was that more than half of the people who had committed suicide did not have any known mental health conditions. Not to mention, prevention has been elusive, even as the rates of psychiatric treatment and diagnosis have greatly increased.

What explains this feeling of despondency and an inclination toward surrendering on the battlefield of life? The late-Charles Le Gai Eaton, British diplomat and one of the finest religious scholars of our era, asked another, perhaps more important question: "What is it that makes us so unwilling to look at ourselves calmly and objectively?" I excerpt the answer from his book, *Reflections*:

> Fear, I suppose, and defensiveness. If we admit our weaknesses to ourselves we would—so we think—be weakened in the face of the world and less able to cope with the dangers and the problems that surround us; and, if we don't build up our own "image," no one else is going to do it for us. Of what use is a deflated balloon, even if there is a fierce-looking face painted on it? We must blow the balloon up and present that face to the world.
>
> But there's a problem here. The more we try to live a lie, the more vulnerable we become. We're afraid of being caught out by other people; above all, we're afraid of being caught out by ourselves. A lie always needs to be supported by further lies, and then by still more lies, until we find that we have constructed a house of cards that may be blown down at any moment. What happens then? A nervous breakdown, perhaps, or what the psychiatrists call an "identity crisis." Self-deception has its dangers, to say the least.
>
> But, to be able to do without self-deception, we have to feel secure, and, I believe, that this sense of security can come about in only one way. That is from the knowledge that, even here and now, in

this turbulent world, we are living in the presence of God, who sees us objectively, and yet with mercy and loving-kindness. In that all-seeing Presence there is no longer any point in lying or in pretending to be other than we are. This, surely, is what we call "serenity"; to be oneself, to recognize oneself, in the calm certainty that He sees us as we are and accepts us as we are.

The tragedy of modern man, in the midst of his riches and his technological achievements, is that he has lost the sense of the sacred and lives in a world drained of light. Those who have told us, over the past century, that "God is dead" should have had the honesty to complete the sentence: "God is dead, therefore man is dead!" When nothing in our surroundings reminds us of Him, then He does—in a sense—die in our hearts, and all that makes life worth living dies with Him.

The diminishing role of religion, which has long provided the institutional and social scaffolding to establish harmony, balance, and order within the individual personality as in society, is a large factor for our suicide crisis. Studies have shown that suicide rates are lower in religious countries than in secular ones and that people with no religious affiliation perceive fewer reasons for living, here having particularly fewer moral objections to suicide. If nothing else, religion convinces us that there is light at the end of the tunnel, providing meaning and much needed relief from the corroding existential anxiety which afflicts so many people in our time.

"Woe be to a nation which stands far removed from the Truth (God), and hence has died but is not aware of her death," said the poet Allama Iqbal. Breathing-dead bodies on foot, that's what we have become, with no soulful activity. We have sacrificed our spiritual well-being in the name of trivial pursuits, and nothing we have gained in this world—absolutely nothing—can compensate for this devastating loss. In truth, we are spiritual beings having a human experience. The real struggle, then, is the entanglement of the soul in the material world.

From the moment we realize God's scattered signs all around us, we start living in His Divine presence. Our soul discovers itself, and we don't just drag our corpses anymore, but we walk as viceregents of God on earth. Our breathing is no longer evaporation into emptiness, but rather a process to remember God constantly and praise Him under all circumstances. For we know that "with hardship cometh ease."

> *This being human is a guesthouse. Every morning a new arrival. A joy, a depression, a meanness, some momentary awareness comes as an unexpected visitor. Welcome and entertain them all! Even if they are a crowd of sorrows, which violently sweep your house. Still, treat each guest honorably. He may be clearing you out for some new delight. The dark thought, the shame, the malice, meet them at the door laughing and invite them in. Be grateful for whatever comes, because each has been sent as a guide from beyond.*
> — Rumi

*My heart is so small,
it's almost invisible.
How can You place
such big sorrows in it?
"Look," He answered,
"Your eyes are even
smaller, yet they
behold the world."*

— Rumi

The End of Our Time

> *The trouble is, you think you have time.*
> — Buddha

We often think of life in terms of how many years we live. I'm thirty-five today; considering the average life expectancy is about eighty years, the illusion is that I still may have a lot to look forward to. But Tim Urban, author of the blog, *Wait But Why*, has introduced me to a new uncomfortable reality: despite not being at the end of our life, we may very well be nearing the end of our time with some of the most important people in our life.

It turns out that when most of us graduate from high school, we have already used up over 90% of our in-person parent time. During our first eighteen years, we spend some time with our parents for at least 90% of our days. But once we move away for university and then later for work, we probably see our parents an average of two weeks a year—or about 4% of the days we spent with them each year of our childhood. Let's assume we're lucky and that we have twenty more years of coexistence. If the two-weeks-a-year thing holds, that's less than 300 days left to hang with mom and dad.

I work from home and live with my parents (which is quite common in our culture). Thus, this insight helps me appreciate the uniqueness of my situation and to make the most of our remaining face time—not just with my parents, but also my children. Zaynab is five and Fatima is two. Doing the same math gives us about 80% time together over the average lifespan.

Tim also got me thinking about two of my brothers. After living in a house with them for fifteen years, we now live in different countries, and I spend maybe ten days with each of them a year. That leaves us with only 15% of our total hangout time left. The same goes for my old friends. In high school, we did everything together. Now, even though we are scattered around the same city, we all have totally different lives and schedules. The four of us are in the same room probably once a year. The group is in its final 7%.

There are a few takeaways here, as Tim points out.

First, realize how much time has already passed. Otherwise, we will continue to live life unconsciously. As Seneca wrote, "It is not that we have a short time to live, but that we waste a lot of it... Life is long if you know how to use it."

Second, focus on priorities. Everyone hustles life along, but make a list of how you spend your time—and make sure it is how you want it. Time is, after all, the least thing we have of, to quote Hemingway.

Third, quality time matters. If you're in your last 10% of time with someone you love, keep that fact in the front of your mind when you're with them and treat that time as special.

Fourth, if you desire to spend *more* time with the most important people in your life, then make it happen. Putting things off is the biggest waste of life. As Napoleon Hill said, "The time will never be *just* right."

Isn't time—that frustratingly finite, unrenewable resource—the real capital bequeathed unto us? Spend it wisely.

The Dip

Three years ago, I felt like giving up. Mark Twain said, "Write without pay until somebody offers pay; if nobody offers within three years, sawing wood is what you were intended for." I was approaching the end of my third year of writing, and my savings had run out. The business was only generating $40,000 in revenue, so we were living month to month.

My wife had no idea, and we were expecting our second child. I had made a decision not to let her in on the financial realities from the very beginning so as not to worry her. She had married a more prosperous Jawad, and it was important for me that her lifestyle not change one bit. The business was a risk I was taking, so I internalized all the emotional volatility that came with it.

What got me thinking of quitting was when I could not attend the wedding of one of my closest friends in Beirut because I could not afford the airfare. I felt so embarrassed. To this day, I haven't told her the truth. The situation was more dire because I had no idea where money would come from to cover hospital expenses for the delivery of our baby a few months out.

There was nothing more pleasurable I could imagine doing with my time than writing *Stray Reflections*, but my commitment was wavering because my circumstances were changing. I updated my resume, started applying for jobs, and even went to a few interviews. I felt like I was cheating myself, but still, I went through the motions. I had to be responsible.

I didn't have the maturity to know at the time, but that period was, what Seth Godin calls, the Dip, that critical turning point in a life or business when the joys of starting have faded and the proverbial "light at the end of the tunnel" is still out of reach. The Dip is the set of artificial screens set up to keep people from going to the next level and realizing their true potential. As Godin states:

> You get what you deserve when you embrace the Dip and treat it like the opportunity that it really is. If you can keep going when the system is expecting you to stop, you will achieve extraordinary results. The people who make it through the Dip are scarce, so they generate more value. For whatever reason, they refuse to abandon the quest and they push through the Dip to the other side. The focus is rewarded by a marketplace in search of the best in the world. The Dip is the secret to your success.

I felt like I was beaten, but I still believed in what I was doing. "The whole course of things goes to teach us faith," as Ralph Waldo Emerson advised. "There is guidance for each of us, and by lowly listening, we shall hear the right word. We need only obey."

What I heard was that it's not all for nothing. That surviving is, in fact, succeeding. I was making progress and only had two choices: quit or be exceptional. I chose the latter. As Godin writes, "In a competitive world, adversity is your ally. The harder it gets, the better chance you have of insulating yourself from the competition."

I gave up the search and invested all of my time, energy, and effort in the business. I used the Dip as an opportunity to get better every single day. I started writing more, traveling more, and building a community and an experience that people wanted to be a part of. This way, I took risks and focused on branding while everyone else was busy selling. I'm happier playing the long game. It's sensationally more powerful.

After persevering through the Dip, I told my wife everything. Her reaction was priceless. "So, wait, we didn't have any money?" Her eyes showed fear and guilt, and then, as she realized all this was in the past, she breathed a sigh of relief and a smile broke across her face. We laughed together.

A story takes time to unfold.

The best way out is always through.
— Robert Frost

Memento Mori

> *Remembering that I'll be dead soon is the most important tool I've ever encountered to help me make the big choices in life. Almost everything—external expectations, pride, fear of embarrassment or failure—these things just fall away in the face of death, leaving only what is truly important.*
> — Steve Jobs

"You may not wake up tomorrow." Seneca urged us to tell ourselves this when going to bed. And when waking up, to say, "You may not sleep again." To keep death at the forefront of our thoughts, he believed, would reveal the true insignificance of some of our worries and bring thoughtfulness into all aspects of life. He went on to say, "Let us prepare our minds as if we have come to the very end of life."

The inevitability of death doesn't make life pointless, but rather, it makes it purposeful. "You could leave life right now," Marcus Aurelius wrote in *Meditations*. "Let that determine what you do and say and think." It happens that in thinking about death, we are also thinking about life: what matters, what needs to change, what we must accept, and what we should let go. In a way, death is an organizing principle, helping to account for our life in an honest way. Very few things stand up when measured against the finality of death. As Don Juan suggests, take death as your advisor.

To remember death isn't to be morbid: it is to remember that we are mortal, that our time on earth is finite and short. Azrael can come for us at any time, any moment. Imam al-Ghazzali said the thought should elicit a response or a reaction in accordance with the evolution of each person. If one is deeply attached to the material world, he or she remembers death and loathes it, fearing the deprivation of its pleasures. If dying instills fear, the spiritual reward for this is immense if we become firmer in repentance and devotion. Only the remembrance of the knower brings calm and peace. He or she has reached the station of contentment and surrender by turning attention toward the immortality of the soul.

Mindfulness of death is a central teaching in all spiritual traditions. "Of all meditations, that on death is supreme," said Buddha. The meditative practice *marana-sati*, meaning "death awareness," is considered essential to extricate ourselves from our exclusive preoccupation with the world. The Prophet Muhammed (PBUH) called upon people to visit graveyards to think about death and consider one's mortality. "The wisest among you is he who remembers death the most," he said, "and the most prudent is he who is the most prepared for it." Shakespeare said that every third thought should be of our grave.

I can't say that I'm ready to stare death in the face, but I do think often about life's impermanence. It is why I don't hold any grudges, why I'm ready to make up with my wife soon after a big fight, why I don't take my time with my children for granted, why I don't sweat the small stuff, why I worry less about the future, why I am supercharged with even more ambition, why I desire no more than what is necessary, why I spend some time in seclusion, why I'm filled with so much gratitude, and why I see only my own mountain of weaknesses. In short, you could say to practice dying is to practice being a better person.

There is even an app, WeCroak, to help build a regular practice of contemplating mortality; the app is inspired by a Bhutanese folk saying that to be a happy person, one must contemplate death five times a day. Therefore, each day, at random times and at any moment—just like death—you receive this alert: "Don't forget, you're going to die." You can click to read a quote about death, ponder, sit silently, take a deep breath, bask in the now, do something different, or discover something new.

The micro dose of mortality comes from a variety of sources, including the work of Emily Dickinson, Pablo Neruda, Kabir, Henry David Thoreau, Pablo Neruda, Lao Tzu, Margaret Atwood, and even Zoolander, who states, "Did you ever think that maybe there is more to life than being really, really, really, really, really, ridiculously good looking?"

In the end, we all belong to God, and to Him we shall return.

Stray Reflections
by Jawad S. Mian

Designed by Tulip Hazbar

Copyright © Jawad S. Mian 2020
All Rights reserved. No part of this publication
may be reproduced, copied or transmitted
without the permission of the author.

Printed in Great Britain
by Amazon